China's Evolving Consumers

 Intimate Portraits

Edited by Tom Nunlist

EARNSHAW BOOKS

China's Evolving Consumers

Edited by Tom Nunlist

ISBN-13: 978-988-8422-90-6

Cover design: Jason Wong

BUSINESS & ECONOMICS / Consumer Behavior

EB106

Published by Earnshaw Books Ltd. (Hong Kong)

Contents

CONTRIBUTORS

 **Tom Nunlist** has been studying China for ten years, and has lived and worked in Shanghai for five years. As a journalist, he wrote and edited feature stories on economics, policy and business in China. He now works as China analyst for an international risk consulting firm.

 **Ashok Sethi** leads the Illuminera Institute in Shanghai, an organization dedicated to skill-building, consultancy and thought leadership in the area of consumer insights and marketing. Ashok has over 30 years of experience in this field and has been studying Chinese consumers for the last 15 years. Ashok has held a number of senior-level positions including Managing Director of TNS China, Regional Director Methodology and Consumer Insights at TNS Asia-Pacific and Managing Director of GfK China-Consumer Experience.

 **Sacha Cody** is an anthropologist and China Studies scholar living in China. A research-based consultant for many years, Sacha has helped businesses, governments, and NGOs understand Chinese society and culture. In 2016, he completed a doctorate in anthropology at the Australian National University, researching food safety, organic farming and the politics of urbanization and rural development in China. He is currently undertaking ethnographic research into international Chinese businesses.

Zoe Hatten is a doctoral candidate in anthropology at the Australian National University. While based in Shanghai from 2015 to 2017, she conducted ethnographic research exploring the commercialization of marriage in post-Mao China.

Annie Fang is the founder of boutique consultancy firm Nine Dots Solutions, which focuses on helping startups building businesses from zero to one. She also contributes five hours of work per week as a therapist, helping veterans from the People's Liberation Army Special Operations Forces adapt to society.

Elisabeth de Gramont has spent the last 12 years traveling across China helping some of the world's biggest brands better understand their consumers. She is the Managing Director of C Space Jigsaw, a leading consumer insight and collaboration agency.

Sizhang Kong is Partner, Research Director and Co-founder of Metis International. She heads Metis Family Research, which focuses on issues surrounding the transformation of women's roles inside the family.

Francesca Hansstein, Ph.D., is an applied statistician currently working at the School of Public Economics and Administration, Shanghai University of Finance and Economics. Her research interests include consumer behavior, analysis and modeling. She also works as a freelancer on China-based market research projects.

Francis Bassolino has been aging in Shanghai for the past thirty years. He runs Alaris, an investment advisory and management consulting firm.

Forrest Cranmer is a consultant working for Alaris Consulting. He has a background in economics and Chinese studies, and is a fluent speaker of Mandarin.

ACKNOWLEDGEMENT

This book would not have been possible without Frank Tsai, who Graham Earnshaw, founder of Earnshaw Books, likes to call "The Great Connector" of Shanghai. Through the vibrant community of intellectuals and professionals Frank has built with his long-running, sometimes raucous, and always stimulating lecture series, we were able to find a group of contributors even more talented than they are diverse. Frank's numerous lecture series, including *China Crossroads* and *Hopkins China Forum*, his writings and more can be found at *www.shanghai-review.org*.

OVERVIEW

China, for Western Brands, is Changing

Tom Nunlist

FOREIGN CONSUMER BRANDS have more to gain in China than ever before, and a greater need than ever to understand the Chinese consumer. But the consumer landscape is changing fast, and analysis tends to focus only on numbers and market-wide generalizations. This book takes an in-depth look at the lives of Chinese consumers, largely from the middle class, in order to gain a more personal, human understanding of the world's biggest consumer growth story.

In 2016, China's private consumption reached $4.4 trillion, according to Morgan Stanley. That's more than double the roughly $2 trillion spent in 2010, and almost seven times the $650 billion spent in 2000. But the real eye-popping figure is how much room there is left to grow—to give you an idea, US consumer spending in 2016 was $15.4 trillion, and that's with a population less that one-quarter the size of China.

It will take Chinese consumers a long time to match their counterparts in the US, but the shorter-term horizons are inviting. By 2021, consumption in China is projected to be $6.1 trillion, and there will be growth across many sectors. In 2016, China's car market grew by 13.7% to more than 28 million vehicles—about 1/3 of the world's total 77 million sales—and KPMG anticipates 33 million annual sales by 2030. China's newly-affluent consumers are developing new tastes, importing over 100,000 tons of cheese products from 10 major cheese-producing countries in 2016, much of it paired with 642 million bottles of imported wine. Sales of so many items are exploding: the disposable diaper market, to go straight to the bottom of the issue, grew from just over $2 billion in 2009 to over $7 billion in 2016. Business intelligence consultancy Euromonitor International predicts the market to top $10 billion in 2019.

The core consumers driving this growth, what we term China's "New Middle Class," have been the subject of reams of breathless analysis describing the money to be made from them. But most of the material published misses the other half of the story: those same consumers are evolving, and along with the added pressures of increased competition, it is getting more difficult to reach them.

Take China's $190 billion fast-moving consumer goods (FMCG) market, for example. While foreign brands grew sales by 1.5% in 2016, domestic Chinese brands expanded sales by more than 8%. In today's most important growth segment, the premium market, which can include such things as upmarket bottled water and extra-soft toilet paper, foreign brands lost market share in 18 of 26 FMCG categories, according to a survey of 40,000 households by Bain and Kantar Worldpanel, which specialize in management consulting and consumer research respectively.

Not only is marketing more difficult in today's China, but also far more is at stake. When foreign brands first began making in-roads into China, the country was an uncharted frontier marketplace that held the promise of discovering a "New World." No one was sure what they were doing, and so gambles tended to be small. Today, the China market is vital to almost any international company and many top brands already have billions of dollars invested here.

Success for any brand depends precisely on keeping up with China's fast-evolving consumers. In order to not lose out, brands must have a clear understanding of who they are selling to, and the forces that are shaping them. To that end, this book takes an intimate look at eight different types of people mostly from China's "New Middle Class" that are driving change—men and women, young and old, reasonably well-off and quite rich.

But before taking the deep dive, it is important to get an overview.

Newly Prosperous, Broadly Speaking

As a term, the "New Middle Class" is imperfect—it carries much baggage from the Western context, and so can be misleading. Simply put, it refers to Chinese people with at least enough leisure time and spending power to be able to seriously consider lifestyle choices. The vast majority of them are urbanites, as opposed to countrysiders or transplants. In some ways this group resembles the Western middle class, which explains the use of the term itself. They have the means to take vacations, collectively spending $261 billion in 2016 according to the United Nations World Tourism Organization. Goldman Sachs predicts them to be spending $450 billion vacationing overseas by 2025. They enjoy the ambiance of a coffee shop enough to support over 2,000 Starbucks locations in more than 100 cities, not to mention all of Starbucks' competitors both foreign and domestic. The upper end of the group sent more than 300,000 of their children overseas to school in 2015, contributing $9.8 billion to the US economy alone.

Considering the sheer size of this group—146 million according to Goldman Sachs—it is easy to become wide-eyed and miss deeper truths. The fact is, this so-called "New Middle Class" is not really in the "middle" of anything. (Note: There are many competing numbers as to the size of China's middle class, the point of disagreement mainly being the salary threshold. The Goldman Sachs estimation, the one we consider to be most correct, is at the lower end, using an average annual income of nearly $12,000. At the higher end is the estimation by the Center for Strategic and International Studies, a respected US think tank, which puts the number at 420 million people. But this includes individuals making $10 a day, or $3,650 annually. At such a salary, even a comparatively simple Starbucks latte would be half a day's wages. While allowing for some flexibility, for example fresh college graduates are typically paid in this range, we do not consider this to be a middle-class income.)

In domestic terms, they are much closer to being an elite, making up only a bit more than 10% of the total population, and are only about a quarter of the urban population. Even in China's quite posh top-level cities—Beijing, Shanghai, Guangzhou and arguably a few others—one can easily stroll from deluxe to dilapidated, even in central areas of town, in just a block or two. Car ownership, a hallmark of middle-class prosperity the world over, is similarly revealing: at the end of 2015, car ownership reached 172 million, or 31 cars for every 100 households, according to China's Ministry of Public Security. In the US, by contrast, more than 90% of households have at least one car, and more than half own two or more. Although abject poverty is largely a thing of the past in China, 623 million Chinese people have an annual per capita income of less than $6,000, also according to Goldman Sachs, which leaves little room for discretionary spending.

But if in their own country they are at the top of the heap, China's New Middle Classers are closer to the bottom compared to developed countries. Only about 15% of China's working population earns more than RMB 80,000 ($11,700) annually, which is just below the $12,060 poverty line in the US for a single person with no dependents. There is of course quite a bit more context that can be provided for those numbers, starting with cost of living—according to Numbeo, a crowd-sourced database of global consumer prices, consumer prices in the US are 69% higher than in China—but the rough comparison does indeed give a rough idea.

Still, as far as Chinese people are concerned, the far more important comparison is the domestic one. People that can be counted among this "New Middle Class" are living lives of comfort and choice almost unimaginable even 20 years ago. That means radical changes for the diversity of people that fall into this broad income-based category. Living memory in China easily covers both ration coupons and iPhones. What constitutes "success" in life no longer necessarily includes traditional ideals of family harmony—having "three generations under one roof," for example. Instead, the "ideal life" today has a less strict definition. Traditional and modern ideas coexist, possibilities have multiplied and competition has increased.

Eight Consumers

In this book, we explore how these shifting realties have shaped the lives, attitudes and choices of Chinese consumers. This includes what drives purchasing decisions on a level deeper than simply *preference*.

Developing compelling brands and products means much more than simply keeping up with shifting tastes and emerging trends, but truly understanding the target audience. To clarify things, we have generated an understanding of eight key groups of people. We look at where they come from, and where they want to go; their aspirations and fears; the challenges that they have put behind them and the new pressures they now face. More fundamentally than figuring out what they buy, we aim to figure out *who they are*.

Despite the superficial truth that Chinese people now live "more comfortable lives," the actual process of updating values and transforming long-held traditions is for many uncomfortable. For the urban elderly, it means figuring out what to do in old age, even facing the prospect of a retirement home, a concept once alien to China. For busy married adults, it means reconciling the expectations of long-held traditions with the realities and opportunities of the 21st century. For the young just tasting the freedom and weight of adulthood, it means navigating a culture that is more complex than ever before, not to mention an economy that is transforming even as it is slowing down. For women who choose career over family, it means pursuing one ideal at the expense of another. Revealingly, the 2017 World Happiness Report, published by the United Nations, ranked Mainland China 79 out of 106 countries surveyed, behind troubled nations like Libya (68) and El Salvador (45).

These people are all consumers, and their acts of consumption fulfill complex needs defined both by the world they live in and the identities they forge for themselves. Be it cosmetics or a car, a handbag or a snack—no purchase is simply a purchase but, on one level or another, also an act of expression, as is the case everywhere in the world. What is different from the West, though, is everything else, sometimes in massive and obvious ways, and other times in subtle ways that might escape attention. The key to success in the promotion of brands and products is to as much as possible put yourself in the shoes of the buyer.

In this book, we try on eight pairs of shoes, as it were. Individually, each chapter aims to create an impression of the lives of each type of consumer, each type of person. Taken together, they provide a basic topography of China's "New Middle Class" consumer landscape. In reading the book, you will get a sense of what life is like for prosperous Chinese people living in the late 2010s. We don't pretend to be providing answers on how to develop your brand in China. But we do provide the intellectual and emotional basis for smart and incisive questions.

CHAPTER ONE

The Wealthy and Evolving "Tuhao"

Sacha Cody

"WHO ARE *tuhao*? What is *tuhao*?" Whenever I asked these and similar questions to colleagues, friends and interviewees in China, a wry smile inevitably appeared on their faces. "Oh, *tuhao*," they would say, "let *me* tell you about *tuhao*!" And off they would go... But no one would admit they were *tuhao*, nor even that any of their friends were *tuhao*.

When I asked my colleague Caroline Law, Director of Qualitative Research at Firefly, a global research firm, to outline a "typical" *tuhao*, without hesitation she sketched the image of a Chinese man in his mid-to late-40s—perhaps balding—wearing a Burberry polo shirt, Hermes belt, Gucci leather shoes, a Rolex watch on his arm, gold chain around his neck, and a bright national-flag-red packet of Zhonghua cigarettes—personal favorite of Mao Zedong, costing RMB 100 per box as opposed to the more typical RMB 10—packed neatly into a leather man-bag tucked snuggly beneath his upper arm.

"*Tuhao* are rich, but they have no taste," Law explained. "Whether for a meal, a set of clothes or an apartment, or even a car, they pay for everything in cash."

In fact, amongst most of the people I spoke with—who,

like Law, live in China's coastal cities and were born in the 1970s and later—*tuhao* are an altogether unique breed of individual. They are older, hail from provincial capitals inland and, as this description shows, there is something both shady and yet comical about them.

To be more precise, *tuhao* (土豪) refers to a group of Chinese (mainly men from outside China's first-tier cities) who became rich by "jumping into the sea" of business in the 1980s and early 1990s, when entrepreneurialism was reemerging in China. At the time, this was still a bit disreputable, and absolutely uncertain both in terms of chances for success and the basic methods of deal-making. Often these entrepreneurs cleverly leveraged government relationships to buy public assets cheaply and profit handsomely. They took advantage of market asymmetries and the first wave of opportunities to profit from reform and opening policies.

Very roughly speaking, the term connotes the "new rich," and in most contexts is a playfully derogatory term. It often refers to people with self-acquired, rather than inherited, wealth, enabling them to rise in social status. Having only recently become members of the moneyed class, many people (often "old money," but also younger people who came of age with a mass-media education in "taste") believe that these "new rich" lack the civility, taste and personal cultivation required to fulfill the responsibilities their new social status demands. They also have an air of buffoonery, trying to fit in but unable to conceal their origins. As such, the consumption practices of these new rich have become the subject of ridicule—they are mocked as coarse, crude, ostentatious, tasteless, tawdry, vulgar... the list goes on.

Writing in America at the end of the nineteenth century,

economist and sociologist Thorstein Veblen used the polite term "pecuniary emulation" to refer to the spectacular failure of the new rich to model more seasoned money, and there is something of a comparison to be made with China today. Similarly in 1990s Russia, a group of business people (mainly men) made their fortunes by taking advantage of government connections following the collapse of the Soviet Union. Labeled the "New Russians," they were known for flaunting their wealth with expensive gold jewelry and driving conspicuous luxury cars. Consider, however, rap and hip-hop music in the United States; protagonists who have crafted an image of themselves as individuals who rhyme their way off the streets and into fame and fortune, giant gold chains, and champagne-soaked parties. The trope of absurd wealth has existed since the early days of rap, and, uniquely, has become codified into the rap genre in ways that are hilariously self-referential. Atlanta, Georgia rap trio Migos scored a major hit in 2017 with "Bad and Boujee" (as in "bourgeois"), the video of which features many jewelry-clad, champagne-sipping young vixens delicately eating fried chicken in a Southern-style diner with fine silverware.

Culturally speaking, the essence of *tuhao* hinges on whether or not one comprehends the so-called "rules of the game." Zhao Fujia, a wealthy and intelligent businessman also enrolled in a doctoral program in political science in Shanghai, explained: "*Tuhao* just don't *get it* when it comes to money. They're out of touch."

This seems to hold true even for those that have reached the ranks of the global rich. Zhao points out that Wang Jianlin, the billionaire founder and Chairman of Dalian Wanda

Group, China's largest and now-troubled real estate developer and the world's largest movie chain operator, smacks of *tuhao*. In a speech in 2016, he offered the following financial advice: "You shouldn't be that ambitious. Set a small target first, like earning 100 million *yuan* ($15 million)." Wang was roundly castigated by a nation of people who have mastered Internet memes, if not the art of the deal. Wang was one of the first to profit from China's property market back when it was a novel idea. This required bravery, a willingness to take risks and the ability to foster government relations. Netizens, however, see shadiness and *tuhao*-ness rather than an exemplary role model.

The disconnect does not need to be quite so epic, though. I interviewed Zhao Fujia at his 250 square-meter apartment overlooking the Bund in Shanghai. Certainly one of the most exclusive locations in the entire country—the average selling price per square meter is RMB 200,000 ($30,100) ten times the city average and double the New York average—Zhao had decked out his palatial home with marble floors, a Japanese-style room for conversing with guests over tea, and expensive furniture and art from all over the world. And yet he apologized profusely that we could not conduct our interview sitting on the couch because the wrong model had been shipped from Italy and he had just sent it back. It was an understandable situation, to be sure, but equally over the top. Although Zhao and I both knew we were poles apart on the socioeconomic ladder, he couldn't help but pretend that this gap didn't exist or matter, treating his luxury furniture (or lack of it) as an inconsequential conversation starter to "break the ice." So instead, we sat down to chat at his 16-seat dining table.

Nonetheless, when it comes to China, equating *tuhao* with, and translating it as, "new rich" is misleading. It conceals the historical and contemporary cultural context, which is important. Nearly all of China's wealth is "new" anyhow, as a lot of "old money" was wiped out during the Communist Revolution in 1949, and then later the Cultural Revolution. Moreover, while *tuhao* seem to present businesses with a stereotypical and easy target—"sell them expensive stuff they can show off"—this chapter aims to show that things are not so straightforward. Today, China's rich are less likely to be *tuhao*. They seek subtlety and experiences rather than crass displays of wealth. Their motivations and anxieties are changing.

Origin Stories

Let us indulge in a brief etymological exploration of the term *tuhao*, which is in fact very old. Literature from the Northern and Southern Dynasties (the fifth and sixth centuries CE) reference *tuhao* as the landed gentry in China's countryside. Landed gentry were degree holders in China's Confucian imperial academic system that were not granted a government position (there were between 30 and 40 degree holders for every position available). These intellectuals often returned to their hometowns and fulfilled social functions such as tending to local disputes and collecting taxes. *Tuhao* were thus a local authority in the countryside: *tu* (土) which can connote "rural," and *hao* (豪) which means "power and authority." They held positive, or at least neutral, positions in Chinese society. During Republican China (1911–1949) the Nationalist government prioritized the city over the countryside, siphoning tax money and grain from the farms to the city. *Tuhao* were of little use to the government, and quickly became old-fashioned and outdated. Today's official translation of *tuhao*, "local despot," is ideologically infused—it emerged following the Communist Revolution and the strong peasant support base the Chinese Communist Party built. Wealth was demonized and landowners became the sworn enemies of The People. Today, the term is also a sly dig by urban sophisticates at perceived *nouveau riche* hicks, as the word *tu* also has the strong connotation of "uncultured."

Of course, attitudes toward wealth have changed dramatically in China since the death of Mao Zedong in 1976. The wealthy class in China today, be they educated elite, successful entrepreneurs or senior executives, are no longer the scorn of the CCP but are part of the backbone of the economy, both as producers and consumers. And after nearly forty years of state capitalist experimentation, there are many of them around, although proportionally fewer than in many other economies, given China's large population. According to investment bank Credit Suisse's *2016 Global Wealth Report*, there are 33 million adults with wealth in excess of $1 million across the world. Approximately 5% of them live in China, or 1,590,000 people (0.11% of China's own population)—this compares to the US (home to 41% of the world's millionaires), Japan (9%), the UK (7%), France (5%) and Germany (5%).

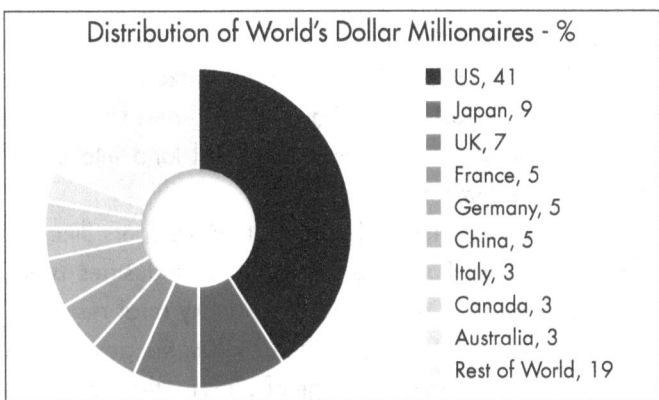

Distribution of World's Dollar Millionaires - %

- US, 41
- Japan, 9
- UK, 7
- France, 5
- Germany, 5
- China, 5
- Italy, 3
- Canada, 3
- Australia, 3
- Rest of World, 19

Distribution of world's 33 million US Dollar millionaires
Source: Credit Suisse Global Wealth Report 2016

Perhaps somewhat surprisingly, the number of millionaires in China has recently declined. In 2015 there were 43,000 more than in 2016. This decline may be due to emigration, declining wealth or various other reasons. In representing Ultra High Net Work Individuals—those which Credit Suisse defines as having $50 million or more—China does a bit better, with 7% of the global population, or 11,000 people (almost doubling from 2015 to 2017). By contrast, the US is home to more than half of these, the world's fattest cats. But China isn't doing so bad.

Earnin'

How did China's 1,590,000 rich make their money? The *Hurun Report*, an annual ranking of China's 100 richest individuals and families, provides insight into this question. Real estate, without doubt, is the prime source of wealth—35% of China's richest individuals and families have earned all or a significant part of their wealth through real estate. This correlates with China's large-scale urbanization. In the early 1950s, only 13% of China's population was urban, but by 2015, it was 56% and is expected to reach 70% by 2050. This speed of urbanization, which is four to six times faster than that of the US and UK, was in part achieved by reclassification of rural land into urban land for development.

Naturally urbanites and real estate developers (like our billionaire Wang Jianlin) and associated industries profited handsomely, but so too did a few lucky rural residents. Throughout the 1980s and into the 1990s, the government compensated farmers at the edge of cities for their land with either cash or a modern high-rise apartment, and sometimes both. While many were cheated or bullied out of their fair share and have been featured in the media over the years, some did better, relatively speaking. A rural farmer who eked out a living on a few thousand RMB a year who suddenly has two or three million RMB in his or her pocket (approximately $300,000 to $440,000) may behave similarly to a Western middle-class resident who wins the lottery jackpot. There are stories of rural residents following the government purchase of their land going on spending sprees of cars, properties, luxury clothes and gold jewelry. Perhaps finding bank accounts too conservative an option, and maybe not appreciating the concept of depreciation, they might "invest" in items that have an immediate sense of value to them.

Today, as this process continues, having property bought out by the local government is a dream for many. In the twenty-first century, urban land has become even more valuable. Living in Beijing in the early 2000s, my first landlord owned two shanty houses outside the East Second Ring Road, just a few kilometers from the Forbidden City. In order to maximize compensation owed once the government bulldozed their homes to make way for modern residential compounds, my landlord and his wife lived separately—a condition of receiving compensation was that all apartments were fully occupied at the time of demolition. They did very well for themselves. In 2017, a friend who had purchased a commercial property for RMB 2 million several years previously sold it for RMB 70 million to a developer. This friend is what is called a *chaierdai* (拆二代), "rich through demolition," a new generation and sub-group of *tuhao*.

"Investments" are the second largest source of wealth according to the *Hurun Report*, with 24% of China's richest individuals and families earning all or a significant part of their wealth from investments. Taking Mr. Zhao as an example, his business interests are diverse. He and his family together run a successful eyeglasses business across China and northeast Asia, a day-spa and health-and-wellness business in Canada, and now a newly-founded third business, importing premium brand goods from Europe into China for babies and pregnant women. Zhao is sitting on a potential gold mine. In 2016, 176,000 metric tons of infant formula powder was imported into China, with the EU contributing the largest share. Premium imported milk powder runs at about $30 a kilo (although sometimes much more if there is a shortage).

Other important sources of wealth include IT (10%), entertainment and culture (9%), mining and metals (9%), pharmaceuticals (9%), finance and related services (8%), digital industries including online gaming and e-commerce (7%) and energy (7%).

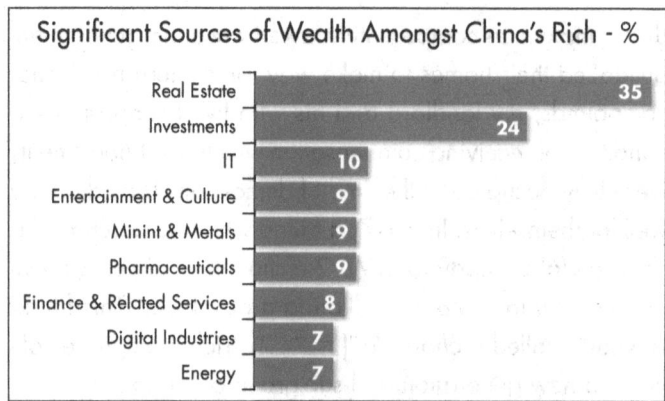

Significant sources of wealth amongst China's rich
Source: Hurun Report 2016

Some of these other sources of wealth are a sign of things to come. According to Millward Brown, a global consultancy specializing in brand, media and communications research and strategy, China's strongest global brands are split between "traditional" businesses such as Lenovo, Huawei and Air China, and a new breed of Internet and digital businesses including Alibaba and Tencent.

Alibaba shot to notoriety in September 2014 when it began trading on the New York Stock Exchange, raising $25 billion for the company and investors in what was the largest initial public offering in US history. Charismatic Jack Ma, who now speaks to world leaders about globalization at events like the World Economic Forum and once worked as a free English tour guide in Hangzhou when he was young, founded and leads Alibaba Group, a family of Internet-related businesses comprising wholesale and retail marketplaces as well as support services provided by ecosystem participants (including financial services, logistics, and media and entertainment). In addition to brains and commercial brawn, timing and choice of industry also explain Ma's charisma and stellar status across China. Unlike billionaire Wang Jianlin who earned his money in the early days of reform through possibly shady real estate deals, Ma's first success came later when he built an Internet platform that millions of other small Chinese businesses could also profit from. Not many would call Ma a *tuhao*.

Spendin'

But *tuhao* are known less for being rich *per se* than they are for spending money and letting everyone know how luxurious their lives are. The amount of retail selling space dedicated to luxury in China is second only to the US, and in 2016, China accounted for over one-third of the global luxury spend of $1.2 trillion. Luxury spending, even at such a scale, is not necessarily crass, but the breed of vulgarity Ms. Law pointed out is easy to find—not least because it seeks to be visible. A few years ago, for example, local media in southeastern Anhui province reported an intriguing story about a wedding between the daughter of a wealthy mining magnate and the son of "normal salaried class" parents. According to local media, the groom was so handsome he won over the mother-in-law, who gifted him a Bentley automobile worth RMB 4 million ($600,000). On receipt, the groom knelt down in front of all the guests, promising to spend his entire life never disappointing the bride. Netizens reared their sarcastic heads immediately; rather than struggle and strive for wealth and success, one netizen posted, just find a "local tyrant" mother-in-law and all your problems will be solved!

Comments such as this, however, are really judgments

from the middle-class, the "normal salaried class." They have toiled hard for much less and believe that China's rich actually have cheated and lied their way to wealth. The comment above is indicative; it implies that anyone who did well from mining *must* be a "local tyrant." It's inconceivable that mining magnates could also be philanthropists or benevolent in some way.

There is certainly some truth to these accusations. Minxin Pei, a professor at Claremont McKenna College in the US, wrote about a new era of collusive corruption in China in his recent book *China's Crony Capitalism: the Dynamics of Regime Decay*. Crony capitalism, says Pei, is when entrepreneurs and politicians collude so the former profits financially and the latter profits through retaining and expanding his or her power base. The immense popularity of the 2017 TV series *In the Name of the People* (*Renmin de Mingyi* 人民的名义)—a drama about the hunt for corrupt officials told over 55 episodes—shows the fascination and obsession the average Chinese citizen has with calling out and punishing "local tyrants."

Yet despite the shadiness that looms over many businesspeople and politicians from industries linked to China's early "reform and opening up" period, it is important to understand the deep social and cultural factors that influence and even dictate how the rich spend their money.

For Chinese male entrepreneurs, for example, recognition and the projection of masculinity drive spending habits. John Osburg, an anthropologist at the University of Rochester in the US, spent several years in the late 2000s ethnographically immersed in the world of elite entrepreneurs in Chengdu, Sichuan, in China's southwest. The findings in his book

Anxious Wealth: Money and Morality Amongst China's New Rich are important. Chinese entrepreneurs rely on *renqing* (人情), meaning "human relationships"—but implying more—with government cadres and underworld bosses to facilitate deal making. Their display of wealth is in fact a key means of creating mutual trust and perceptions of reliability. According to Osburg, some Chinese entrepreneurs say of their professions that "entertainment is my job," and they really mean it. Banqueting and the gifting of luxury items (amongst other spending habits) are necessary to create and maintain "lasting networks of mutual aid." And such dynamics can lead to an odd kind of "inflation." Entertaining government cadres central to a deal, for example, moves from a nice restaurant to a lavish banquet room and finally to a massage room. The gift of a Rolex watch becomes the gift of an Audi automobile—although it is important to note that these "traditions" have been greatly impacted in recent years by Xi Jinping's anti-corruption campaign, even to the point of significantly impacting sales of luxury goods in China.

Such gift inflation is not limited to big deal makers. Surprisingly, Apple's launch of the gold-colored iPhone 5s in 2013, with a price tag of RMB 8,800, was a big hit. Soon after launch, a wedding host in the coastal city of Ningbo, Zhejiang province, gifted each of her 80 guests with one. This gesture quickly spawned new terminology amongst netizens; *tuhao jin* (土豪金), or "tuhao gold," quickly evolved from a description of a gold iPhone into a euphemism for extravagance; gold-plated luxury cars and extravagant interior designs—even the *People's Daily's* new office tower in Beijing, which is undeniably phallic in addition to being conspicuously gold—all became *tuhao jin.*

In fact, the enduring popularity and use of the term *tuhao* today—in the face of a declining number of Chinese who really are, in the original sense of the term, *tuhao*—owes itself to Chinese netizens penchant for creative deformation of their language and a pleasure in poking fun at social groups. In the 2010s, online gamers who won not because of their skill in gaming but because they bought up all the gaming items needed to win, were mocked as *tuhao.* Then, in the two months of September and October 2013, coinciding with the gold iPhone launch, over 100 million references to *tuhao* were recorded throughout China's social media universe. The source of this buzz was a joke on *Weibo*, a popular micro blogging site similar to Twitter. So it is told: a rich but unhappy man goes to a Buddhist monk for advice. The man expects the monk to advise him to leave his material life and seek solitude for contemplation. Instead, when the monk learns how much money the man has, he holds out his hand and says *"Tuhao*, let's be friends!" Implying, of course, that gold glitters even for the ascetic.

More recently, the term *tuhao* has evolved to encompass not only the actually rich, but also the purchasing decisions of everyday people—spending money spontaneously can also be *tuhao.* Another of my interviewees, Ms. Lang, pointed this out to me. Lang was born in Beijing, grew up in Hong Kong, and has spent three decades helping firms navigate Chinese cultural nuances as a public relations specialist. She explained that when a middle-class white-collar worker in Shanghai earning RMB 10,000 per month pays for an RMB 8,000 meal for all her friends one evening, this is also *tuhao*. And although in this case it takes more the form of good-natured ribbing, there is still a certain sting to it, and it revolves around the changing relationships between wealth, taste and morality that are influencing ideas about consumption in China.

A Bumpy Ride: from Display to Experience

Perhaps influenced by gift "inflation" and public mockery, there is a change underway in what China's rich spend their money on. Added Value, a global research consultancy specializing in cultural brand strategy, observes a shift from the display of wealth and purchase of things, to the enjoyment of wealth and pursuit of meaningful experiences. Panos Dimitropoulos, an independent artist and also a semiotician—someone who studies the patterns and meanings of cultural signs and symbols—at Added Value, says "Everything is changing in China. Subtlety is replacing scale; color is replacing gold; cultural confidence is replacing blunt nationalism; minimalism is in; exclusive experiences are in; naturalness is in." This means putting some skin in the game; it is not enough to simply display wealth, you have to actually know something about what you are consuming.

This has led to a rush toward cultivating connoisseurship amongst China's wealthy. One of the most noticeable trends is the increased consumption of goods associated with "taste" and "class," such as red wine. How successful China's wealthy are in cultivating taste, however, remains an open question. The 2013 documentary *Red Obsession* discusses how wine makers in the Bordeaux region of France, the wine producing capital of the world, feel threatened by numerous "capricious elements" such as the weather, the global economy and, surprisingly, China. It is not about whether they can keep up with demand, but whether demand from China will fundamentally change the cultural and business landscape in Bordeaux. Warwick Ross, a co-director and co-writer of the documentary and a wine-maker in Australia, believes everyone in China has wine fever. Stampede seems a more apt description; there is little subtlety in China's wine market. In fact, the year *Red Obsession* was released, China became the world's biggest red wine market, consuming 1.86 billion bottles. The industry consensus, in both China and France, is that this is just the beginning. Even with price increases, demand exceeds supply. Vintages are being auctioned off at record prices. Christies, the London-based auction house, made headlines in 2011 when a case of red wine was sold to a Chinese bidder for £135,000 ($176,000), three times the expected price. In 2013, an annual charity wine auction held in the Burgundy region of France, raised a record $8.5 million, boosted by bidding from Chinese attendees. And today, Chinese investors go direct to the source, purchasing estates and vineyards. In 2015, the symbolic 100th Chinese-owned Bordeaux chateaux was acquired by billionaire James Zhou, owner of Chinese metal can manufacturer ORG Packaging. Still, Chinese own just over 1% of the 7,000-plus chateaux that dot the Bordeaux region.

The trend in luxury cars also illuminates this trend toward connoisseurship and "insurance" from being called a *tuhao*. Audi, BMW and Mercedes are certainly the most popular mainstream luxury cars on China's roads today; collectively they sold 1.6 million automobiles in China in

2016, a very modest 6% share of total car sales. Beautiful though these cars are, there is little subtlety in their appearance. This applies even more so for super luxury cars like Ferrari and Porsche, both of which are also continuing to expand in China.

What China's wealthy connoisseurs are shifting to now, however, is restraint. Maserati is trying to capitalize on this change in taste. I remember sitting with one of Maserati China's senior executives in a restaurant in Shanghai a few years ago discussing their China strategy. Demand was exceeding supply, and this Italian executive clearly loved his job: "They ask me to sell beautiful cars in China, and that's what I do." In 2016, Maserati sold 12,250 automobiles in China. Reid Bigland, the Global Head of Maserati at Fiat Chrysler Automobiles—who is described by Forbes as "an imposing figure... he's got the physical presence of a body builder"—is bullish on the China market, and expects sales to jump to at least 17,000 vehicles in 2017.

My conversation with Maserati's China executive quickly turned to the "typical" Maserati customer. "Maserati is all about restraint," the executive said, "and this is what our customers look for."

To many of us, having the Maserati trident logo emblazoned on our grill may not quite say restraint. But remember, we are talking about the sentiment of China's wealthy, and to them there is a significant difference between a Maserati and alternatives. China's rich view Maserati not only as a luxury car that drives beautifully, or as exclusive membership of an elite group of discerning people (often men); they believe it implies restraint and connoisseurship in a way that only a select few can recognize. It puts them in the in-group of the in-group. While a cynic would point out that Maserati's "restraint" allows owners to flaunt their wealth in just the same way as a Ferrari does, a Maserati automobile is to its owner what new clothes are to the Emperor; they believe they can drive largely unnoticed and evade the suspicious eyes of the authorities. Ultimately, however, Maserati owners aren't fooling anyone. Dealers can pick a *tuhao* easily. They are the ones who walk in, take a look around for about five minutes, point and exclaim "I'll take that one!" Then they open a suitcase and hand over the cash.

Perhaps the most fascinating way that China's rich spend their money concerns religion and morality. Wenzhou, a port and industrial city in southeastern Zhejiang province, is well known for its sharp local businessmen, success as an export hub for light manufacturing, and tight-knit diaspora communities around the world. Wenzhou is sometimes referred to as the "birthplace of China's private economy," and is home to Juneyao Airlines, one of China's first private airlines, and Jinwen Railway, China's first joint-venture railway company. Historically, Wenzhou was also a center of European missionary activity and today approximately 10% of the population is Christian. Nanlai Cao, an anthropologist from Renmin University in Beijing, spent several years in the mid 2000s ethnographically studying Wenzhou's wealthy Christians. He estimates there are 50,000 Christian entrepreneurs in Wenzhou, many of whom channel their wealth into church projects, including some of the largest private churches in China. These "Christian bosses," as Cao calls them, are also motivated by patriotic concerns, and even today still recall Deng Xiaoping's call to arms in the 1980s to build a socialist market economy with Chinese characteristics. Their wish is not purely commercial; they want China's rise in the economic realm to be accompanied by a rise in the spiritual realm.

A Christian boss Cao interviewed called Brother Jian put it this way: "Based on my personal experience, I feel the most important thing is to have spiritual release and healing and to have a renewed purposed in life. To have (spiritual) influence on society one must pursue a (business) career."

The sentiment puts an entirely different spin on the joke mentioned earlier about the apparently greedy monk happy to make friends with a *tuhao*. In Wenzhou, China's wealthy seem to have found a better balance between their wealth and morality than the connoisseurs who believe red wine and Maserati automobiles can supplement taste. But this trend is not limited to Wenzhou. According to analysis by the *Hurun Report*, amongst China's rich, nine out of ten donate to good causes, five out of ten donate items and materials, while four out of ten get involved themselves and contribute their own labor, such as helping to build houses in poor rural communities. Viewing those numbers in a bit more context, China on the whole is not a charitable nation at all, according to the Charities Aid Foundation, which ranked China 140th—absolute last—in their 2016 World Giving Index. This means that these wealthy and "crass" individuals who do donate money and other items may be more than what they seem.

Fostering a Class with Class

What all this means for domestic and international business targeting China's rich is not an easy question to answer.

There will of course continue to be a lucrative market in China for all manner of luxury goods and services. When it comes to product portfolio, however, changes in taste must be considered carefully. This is especially the case with design, where subtlety, color, and minimalism are more important. Businesses also need to ask what experience their product or service will deliver. Yet while China's wealthy increasingly seek connoisseurship, *tuhao*-ness can still be found fairly easily, and so is still an opportunity. For example, in one recent wine auction, a Chinese bidder in Hong Kong doubled the price with one paddle rise because she said she "lost patience" with the speed of the auction process. Maserati dealerships also aren't very likely to discourage someone with a suitcase of money from buying a $180,000 automobile on impulse.

The Johnny Walker House in Shanghai seems to have had success. Opened in 2011, it is the first House outside Scotland. Each room is designed to introduce and educate members and visitors on characteristics of the product; whiskey glasses hang from the ceiling of the lobby, a miniature model of a whiskey still sits in one room; other rooms showcase some of the earliest distillers in Scotland as well as the history of Johnnie Walker in Asia. One only gets to the bar at the very last room. While there is nothing secret about the House's exclusivity and pretentiousness, it does do a better job facilitating and equipping members with a kind of connoisseurship that is less *tuhao* and more rooted in product experiences.

Businesses also need to inquire into the culturally-informed motivations of China's rich to position their products appropriately. John Osburg found that elite entrepreneurs in

Chengdu—*tuhao* posterboys to many Chinese—were very anxious that their wealth could be taken away at a moment's notice, a fear that Xi Jinping's anti-corruption drive has surely exacerbated. Yet primitive accumulation seems to be a thing of the past. Today's rich are not just worried about losing their wealth, but also not fitting in and becoming the subject of ridicule. This fear is not only because of smart-ass netizens. As Chinese businesses go global, entrepreneurs and executives engage with overseas peers. They might need a new wardrobe, coaching services to interact with local employees, or presentation skills for shareholder meetings. Upskilling services such as these and product experiences that facilitate genuine connoisseurship, such as Johnnie Walker, rather than theatrical performance like a wine auction, are likely to grow because they can reduce the anxiety of not fitting in.

China's rich want to be recognized as a class with "class." Businesses who provide products and services that help China's rich reach that sweet spot will fare well because their customers will no longer need to claim, "I'm not *tuhao*!"

CHAPTER TWO

China's First Born-rich Generation

Zoe Hatten

AT AN EXCLUSIVE luxury dinner in Bordeaux to celebrate the success of a new wine label in China in June 2017, I noticed that the young man seated next to me seemed uninterested in his wagyu steak or his flight of burgundy. He did not make an effort to converse with the other attendees, but instead, like a distracted teenager, scrolled interminably through messages on his smartphone. (Note: Names have been changed to protect the anonymity of interview sources in this chapter.)

I attempted to engage him in conversation, asking where he was from. He said he was from Hong Kong and handed me a business card that read "Deputy General Manager," as if in the hope of ending our exchange so he could go back to his smart phone. He seemed polite but uninterested, with an unmistakable air of confidence and entitlement. "Who is that man?" I discretely enquired later in the evening. "Oh, that is the Deputy General Manager of our wine import company," explained a colleague, then with an eye roll he added "but actually he does nothing, I have never even spoken to him before. His mother is a wealthy elite company investor, that's why he's here. He is a typical *fuerdai.*"

The term *fuerdai*, pronounced "foo-err-dye," kept popping up in conversations during my time conducting anthropological research on urban Chinese society in 2015 and 2016. During one corporate junket I was invited to attend in Nanchang, the capital of Jiangxi Province in eastern China, we were greeted by our host, Wen Sun, a baby-faced twenty something. He was the heir to a family business empire that dealt mainly in property development. He ferried us by speedboat to his private island in the middle of the Gan River where his family had developed a luxurious function center and hotel. Wen spoke perfect English with a vague British accent he had picked up while studying at an elite tertiary institution—the London School of Economics. His fleet of personal vehicles included several Lamborghinis and Audis, mainly "just toys," he explained. I noticed Wen was always accompanied by a stern looking older man, a trusted employee of his father, who seemed to be keeping tabs on all of his interactions like some kind of henchman. Wen was the princeling, the protégé of the family business empire, but he was not the one calling the shots. He was, I was told, most definitely a *fuerdai*.

Fuerdai means "second-generation rich" in Chinese, although you may have come to suspect such a definition. But to really understand the term, from its emergence to its meaning today, it is first necessary to get a grip on China's unique trajectory of economic development in the post-Mao period.

Wealth in China, Briefly

When Deng Xiaoping declared, in 1992, "Let some people get rich first," the reforms he had first set forth in the late 1970s were already beginning to produce that result.

Throughout the 1980s, as centralized state control of the economy began to relax, entrepreneurial activity began to publicly re-emerge for the first time since 1949. Combined with the massive amounts of private capital flowing into China's special economic zones, China became the workshop of the world. As is widely known, the upheaval made a lot of people rich, or *fu*, on a scale, and often in a manner, that was previously unimaginable—both for themselves and for the rest of the world.

Private wealth really skyrocketed in the 1990s, after Deng Xiaoping's "Southern Tour," meant to reinforce economic reforms, when he uttered his judgement on wealth accumulation. Estimates produced by the International Monetary Fund, World Bank and United Nations indicate that in 2000, China's wealth measured in GPD per capita was roughly 17 times what it had been in 1980. And while the standard of living was generally raised across the board, some people really did hit the jackpot. Whether positioned to benefit from government connections, as many were, or just making good on favorable conditions, rags-to-riches stories abound in the recent family histories of today's second-generation rich.

There are countless anecdotes describing the accumulation of sudden wealth that spawned *fuerdai*—just ask anyone in China, they'll know a few. A Chinese friend of mine in her 30s living in Shanghai noted that three billionaires had graduated from the same high school as her out of a class of 50 in a certain third-tier city in Guangdong Province.

"It is one of those cities that I imagine to be like a small town in Europe, with a population under 30,000, but a contemporary art museum that costs RMB 300 million," she said. "These wealthy people came up in the 1990s, when everything resulted in money."

She went on to tell me in more detail about the rise to wealth of her classmate's father. He did not, as is common in Guangdong, start a factory—he raised a rare breed of turtles, a popular local delicacy. Starting out living and working in a humble shack with a tin roof, he became famous for his expertise in raising these turtles, and as wealth in the region increased, his product was in hot demand. He expanded his business and began to invest the profits in real estate.

"As he continued to accumulate wealth, he simply began building new makeshift floors on top of his existing buildings, building higher and higher the richer he became,"she said. That was China in the 1990s.

Big Spending, Generational Change

What to do with this wealth? As anthropologist John Osburg explains in his 2013 thesis about entrepreneurs in China, *Anxious Wealth*, "There was no established bourgeoisie class to emulate." Nor was there any guidebook for how to spend money. The result has sometimes been legendary spending, vulgar displays of wealth—and that image, like the wealth itself, is something inherited.

A browse on Baidu, China's Google, reveals countless sites and blogs offering commentary on the lives of *fuerdai*, replete with pictures of them splashing cash in outrageous fashion— playing poker late at night, lying around in their bedrooms counting piles of cash, or hanging out with a pet dog wearing an Apple watch on each paw. But the *fuerdai* are not always flashing their wealth in such an obscene manner—in fact, gaudy may be a distinct minority in this group—and looking beyond this stereotype will help us understand them better.

Anna, the daughter of a textiles tycoon from Ningbo, agreed to meet me for a series of interviews. At 24 years old, she struck me as worldly and intelligent. She was confident, considerate, and usually dressed in casual street wear. After graduating with an economics degree in the UK, she had returned to Ningbo for a period, and then moved to Shanghai on what she described as a quest for self-discovery and professional development. She began working at an events and entertainment company, but after a year found it unfulfilling and quit. After all, it's not like she needed the money.

"So, just how wealthy do you need to be to be considered a *fuerdai*?" I asked her. After a pause, she replied, "Your assets could be worth RMB 10 million, or RMB 100 million, but if you are a *fuerdai*, it is because the wealth comes from your parents."

This brings us to another important thing to note about *fuerdai*: The way that the term emphasizes the intergenerational nature of wealth is important, especially in the Chinese context.

While "new money," "rich kids," "heirs and heiresses" of fortunes exist all over the world, the intergenerational factor is where we can locate their Chinese counterparts' unique characteristics. Often, the gap between second-generation Chinese rich and their parents is focused in the offspring's existential struggles to find fulfillment and meaning in their own lives. This is compounded by their experiences as consumers, and their visions of ideal lifestyles, which certainly differ drastically from that of their parents in light of rapidly increased arrays of goods and services available on the domestic market, and increased exposure to global culture. For their parent's generation, there were fewer options for spending, and very different social mores.

As Anna went on to divulge: "In Ningbo in the 1980s and 1990s, my father had nothing to spend his money on except prostitutes. There were no cafés or luxury shops. There was just one bread shop and it was a big deal, and it didn't even serve coffee or anything. Also, my father only drove a fairly standard model Audi, though he could have afforded any car he wanted, to keep a low profile."

Often foreign-educated and worldly, *fuerdai* are, for the most part, extremely self-conscious about where their wealth came from. While stories of turtle farmers and the like are plentiful enough, the factors that determined who got lucky was in many cases influenced by who had government connections. Officials were and are often powerful, and their progeny are sometimes described by a closely related term, *guanerdai,* meaning the children of officials.

As a young London School of Economics graduate from Shanghai explained to me over a glass of sparkling wine at the Grand Hyatt Pudong, many *fuerdai* are also *guanerdai.* "Often the two go hand-in-hand, especially in northern China, where official connections are even more important to succeed in business deals than they are in southern China."

While official connections did not account for all cases of sudden wealth accumulation, they did for many, and this has given rise to a certain bitterness in some when faced with conspicuous wealth they do not enjoy themselves.

More often than not, *fuerdai* are well aware of this.

Many of them are also intent on differentiating themselves from their parents simply as a matter of course, as is the case between all parents and children. Three separate interviewees in their 20s and early 30s confessed to me that they could not work in their parent's business empires, and one of them bluntly admitted that he felt he lacked both the business acumen, and the drive to manage the wealth. Others may feel that given the success of their parents, they need to prove themselves in arenas separate from their family influence. And others still may recognize that the China that gave birth to their wealth is already a China of the past.

Anna, for one, experiences all of these issues to some degree. She is acutely aware that the mode of wealth accumulation that saw her parents skyrocket to their current positions is no longer a reality, nor does it fit a vision of herself as an educated, modern, cosmopolitan elite. This results in feelings of insecurity, coupled with a desire to become self-reliant. She explained that recently, during her time in Shanghai, she felt empty and lacking in direction. Her shopping trips to Europe with girlfriends were only periodic distractions from her larger existential dilemma. She was contemplating different options, including beginning post-graduate training in psychology to become a counsellor, a field still largely undeveloped in China. Whilst she had a few investments, including property, she said she was not satisfied, having still not found her calling. She was also aware, however, that these are to some extent problems of privilege. "People who are not wealthy probably do not feel this pressure, they are too busy working to make ends meet," she reflected.

Mirroring Anna's story is that of Charles, the 30-year-old heir to a coal fortune from Xi'an in Shaanxi Province. His father, a successful factory owner, offered him a managerial position in his company, but it turned out he was not cut out for it. In his words, "I do not want to do business the way my father does, and I cannot, even if I wanted to. Things have changed, we have a modern style of business now in China." Charles dreamt of working in fine arts or design, fields associated with an educated class and imbued with a higher status than in mining.

Similarly, Alvin, the ex-boyfriend of a friend in Shanghai, whose parents owned a steel factory, has so much money he can do anything he wants. However, he has a bad relationship with his father, who he believes only cares about money. The only time he speaks to his father is to call him and ask for funds. His parent's marriage failed, and he felt this was a result of the corrupting effect of wealth. Alvin, who describes himself as "a sensitive person, not suited to the business world," went to an international business school in the US, studying a degree he had no interest in at his parents' request, and eventually dropped out. He is not proud of his wealth, and pretended to be middle class while staying in his student dormitory in the US. "He would never buy luxury items in front of his friends. If he really wanted something, he would instead buy it in private," my friend explained.

Evident in all of these accounts is the evolving idea that wealth does not necessarily beget respect, nor bring happiness and fulfillment. Worse, the unearned quality of it for *fuerdai* can make for an emotional burden.

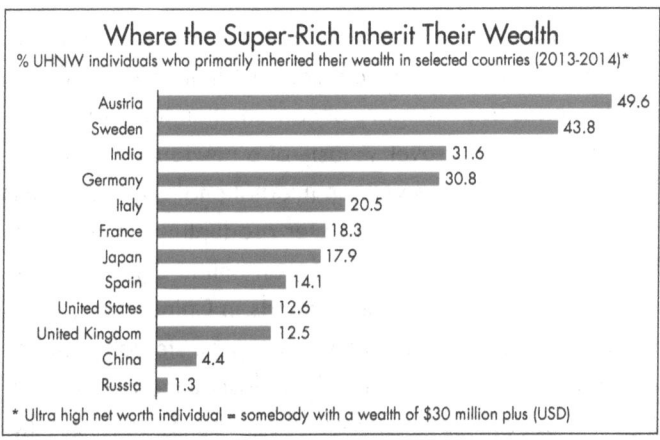

Where the Super-Rich Inherit Their Wealth
% UHNW individuals who primarily inherited their wealth in selected countries (2013-2014)*

Austria	49.6
Sweden	43.8
India	31.6
Germany	30.8
Italy	20.5
France	18.3
Japan	17.9
Spain	14.1
United States	12.6
United Kingdom	12.5
China	4.4
Russia	1.3

* Ultra high net worth individual = somebody with a wealth of $30 million plus (USD)

Inheritance is still a small source wealth in China, but the concept of fuerdai *is nevertheless a very culturally important concept*
Source: Statista

Consumption and China's Global Elite

Two defining factors in the evolution of second-generation Chinese wealth are the rise of information technology and international travel.

An elite overseas education is something that nearly all *fuerdai* I have met have in common, making them the most worldly and mobile generation in China's history. Meanwhile, the rise of the internet has lead to increased options for self-styling, shopping and an overall sense that there is a world beyond China ripe for exploring.

As noted by anthropologist Susanne Bregnbaek in her 2016 book *Fragile Elite, The Dilemmas of China's Top University Students*, aspirations for place of residence constitute a class divide between different levels of elite status and privilege. While a large portion of the Chinese population aspire to a vision of urban success involving established lives in Chinese cities such as Beijing, the super wealthy can choose to live anywhere in the world, and aspire to a version of elite status that is both cosmopolitan and Chinese.

This leads to a category of consumption integral to *fuerdai* as consumers: travel. A taste of a newfound cosmopolitan status often begins with an international education, and while many return to China after graduating, they remain frequent travelers. As *Jing Daily*, an online digital publication covering luxury consumer trends in China reports, Chinese millennial travelers can no longer be stereotyped. The Maldives, Paris and Bali have been fast outmoded by Croatia, the Czech Republic, Antarctica and Burma—destinations recently chosen by some of my own interviewees who were all traveling solo. Domestic exotic locales including Tibet, the wilds of Sichuan, and Inner Mongolia also provide popular backdrops for a newly mobile Chinese elite to live out fantasies of new bourgeoisie-bohemian lifestyles, with new five-star resort facilities popping up in these places to cater to a largely domestic market.

These are not regions with a well-established track record of luxury tourism, but they are places named by several international travel publications as "hot" destinations. So, *fuerdai* are worldly in their travel choices, and not just in a Chinese way. "I want to explore, to find myself," as Mila, a 35-year-old successful restaurateur in Shanghai, told me. She showed me a picture on her smartphone of herself horseback riding in Mongolia wearing a cowboy hat and stirrup boots. Her words reminded me of something straight from the 2010 Hollywood film *Eat, Pray, Love*, in which a glamorous, modern, urban American career woman goes on a spiritual quest for self-discovery throughout Asia, experimenting with a luxurious, new bohemian lifestyle and romantic love affairs.

By the same token, love and marriage is a significant arena of consumption that allows people to show off their elite status. A telling trend in China's wedding industry is the shift from "more is better" to "less is more." It used to be the case that a huge wedding with more guests symbolized more wealth. "Having more guests was just like having more gold bracelets on your arm," a newlywed explained to me. A *fuerdai*, she had rebelled against her parents' wishes for a gigantic wedding. But she spent lavishly all the same, flying a close family group to hold the nuptials on the Greek resort island of Santorini. Upon their return, they had a small celebration in a private Shanghai villa in which they hired "the best jamon carver in China" and served vintage French champagne. The symbolic shift from outrageous fortune to individual taste and status has transformed this all-important rite of passage in Chinese culture.

One thing that is clear from delving into the world of modern China's first born-rich generation is that while some define them by the wealth they inherit, that is not how they want to define themselves. Mila, the successful restaurateur, is perhaps a model of *fuerdai* that many aspire to be. She lives a glamorous, urban lifestyle in Shanghai and is celebrated amongst her peers as being "self-made" and a "taste maker." Her skills and expertise were gained through training in Europe, and she was well-positioned and equipped with the capital to execute her business plan in Shanghai in the mid-2000s. Her own personal accolades have eclipsed the original source of her wealth: her parents factory. That is no longer how she defines herself.

As with Anna from Ningbo, the time and space for travel and reflection mean that *fuerdai* have a unique perspective on their own country that few other Chinese people enjoy. They are, in theory, in a better position than anyone to make good on the unique advantage of capital and experience. With the decline of the middle class in Europe, and the steady rise of domestic consumption in China, *fuerdai* are a class that need to be understood better. We can do this by understanding them not just as consumers, but as people who are increasingly influential members of international society.

CHAPTER THREE

Young, Urban Couples

Ashok Sethi

LI QIANG and Wang Li are married and have known each other nearly all their lives. They are from the same town in Hubei province in central China, studied in the same high school and both travelled to the provincial capital, Wuhan, for university. Born in the 1980s after China implemented its one-child policy, both were supposed to be the only lights in their respective parents' lives, but Wang Li's parents went ahead and had another child, the boy that the society demanded from them, and paid the required penalty.

Wang Li therefore grew up in the company of a much-pampered younger brother, but recalls the play and companionship of her childhood with more fondness than only-child Li Qiang does. After completing their undergraduate degree, Wang Li came to Shanghai to do her Master's. Li Qiang was less keen to pursue further studies but nevertheless accompanied Wang Li to Shanghai and joined the ranks of white-collar workers in the megacity.

Life in Shanghai was not easy with his modest income, but the city's charms were many, and they slowly settled down in the metropolis. Li Qiang was intelligent and dedicated, his employer appreciated his work and rewarded him well, but he soon found even better-paying employment in a multinational company. For the first time in his life, he had money to spend on most, if not all, the things that he desired. After Wang Li acquired her Master's degree, she settled into a job at the university.

Li Qiang and Wang Li feel that they are quite compatible, they share some interests while still having many individual areas of pursuit. Wang Li's parents, having a better economic status than Li Qiang's parents, were less than delighted with their daughter's choice initially, but they slowly learned to accept the boy.

Li Qiang feels that perhaps one of the best financial decisions that he made was to somehow scrape together the money to make the downpayment on an apartment. Although a good 90-minute commute from his office, the apartment is modern and close to his wife's university. Both sets of parents generously chipped in to fund the purchase. They were smart enough to invest in an apartment in Shanghai when such a place was still at the higher end of affordable and often congratulate themselves for having had the wisdom to do so. They see many of their contemporaries burning to buy a place of their own, even as the dream of being a homeowner slowly slips out of reach with ever-rising property prices. It does pinch a bit when they see that they will pay back the mortgage of RMB 20,000 ($3,000) a month for nearly the rest of their working lives, making them feel like *fang nu* (or house slaves). In the initial years, the going was not easy and a large proportion of their salary when to the bank. But Li Qiang's salary has more than doubled since they bought the apartment, and now they are in a better position to enjoy the good things of life.

Both of them believe strongly in education and self-development. They get this from their parents, who always encouraged them to study hard and go to university. They led their lives by this principle, and have extended it to their daughter Niuniu, when she brightened up their lives. Li Qiang went on to acquire a Master's degree in data analytics while still working, a subject that he became more and more interested in and a skill that was also prized in his line of work. Wang Li is more interested in the arts and often tries to acquire new skills or knowledge to enrich her life.

With the birth of the child, the focus on development in her life shifted from self to the child. Wang Li does not like to call herself a "tiger mom," but she diligently shepherds her daughter from piano classes to English classes to museum visits, and tries to make sure that every moment of their interaction contains an element of education. As they are preparing for their daughter's entry to a primary school, they try to make sure that she can already recognize the over five hundred Chinese characters that the school expects her to know even before she begins her formal education.

It is not just Niuniu's mental development that worries them—they are also concerned about her physical health. One of the first things the couple checks on their phone in the morning (after the mandatory WeChat updates) is the Air Quality app. Niuniu's schedule for the day (and to some extent their own) hinges on the reading of AQI (Air Quality Index). They also worry about contamination of food and drink, of which there are shocking examples often reported in the media. With their lives consumed with the task of nurturing their first child, the thought of having another child does not win much favor with them. While some of their friends are already planning a larger family, Wang Li feels that she is too old to have another child, though it would be nice for Niuniu to have some company growing up. Li Qiang would like to have another child, but does not like to make it a bone of contention with his wife.

Li Qiang and Wang Li like to put away at least 20% of what they earn for the future, and the rest they spend, now more and more via online shopping, particularly for their daughter. In fact, scouring the internet for products that are safe and beneficial for Niuniu is a favorite pass-time of Wang Li. This started even before she was born as they went to great lengths to buy German infant milk formula directly from a German store, trying to minimize the chances of ending up with a poor-quality product. Niuniu's stroller, toys and even many of her clothes are bought online, often as a result of the discussions and recommendations from other mothers in the WeChat group that she belongs to. Wang Li feels that she would be quite lost without this group, as her own mother brought her up in a totally different world, and really has little to offer in terms of advice and guidance.

But their online purchases are not just restricted to children's products. Wang Li is keen to use the best skin-care products, as she sees the inevitable signs of aging skin, and often goes for imported luxury brands, sometimes brought in by WeChat *dai gou*—re-sellers—who source or personally bring these products from overseas. Both the husband and the wife buy apparel and shoes online, but Wang Li more so, and more often than not these are stylish and fashionable items, but not luxury brands. The couple is not able to understand the frenzied behavior that some of their richer friends exhibit when it comes to acquiring hand bags and watches. Li Qiang did present his wife with a Coach handbag on her birthday, and Wang Li gifted a Tag Heuer watch to her husband on their tenth wedding anniversary. But apart from these, they tend to shun symbols of ostentatious wealth that they feel are more in line with the tastes and preferences of newly-rich *tuhao* rather than educated urban professionals such as themselves.

However, they do find themselves spending increasingly more on fresh foods, fruits, yogurt, nutritional supplements, sports goods and even red wine. "This is the only life we have and I want to lead it as long and as healthily as possible," Li Quang likes to say. He also feels guilty if he is not able to do a couple of rounds of jogging in the park every day. Wang Li prefers yoga and meditation for her health.

The extent to which they have begun to rely on the internet, particularly through their phones, for all their shopping, their search for safe and healthy products, for recommendations and advice from friends and experts, amazes even them. When they were in the university, there was no Weibo, no WeChat and no Taobao. It was only during their working lives that they slowly found themselves adopting a digital lifestyle, but now nearly all key aspects of their lives—entertainment, social interaction, information seeking and of course shopping—are all digital. They feel it has enriched their lives, and they feel confident that they can handle the deluge of information as well as protect their privacy from those who could exploit it to their advantage.

Tourism and particularly overseas travel is a special indulgence, for which they do wish they had more money than they have now. They first traveled overseas just a year before Niuniu was born. Wang Li's parents also accompanied them. This holiday to Europe exposed them to a new kind of joy, and even a new kind of life, in a place where the air is clean, life is unhurried and where they could bond together and relax in a way they struggle to do when they are in Shanghai. After Niuniu came along, they took short holidays with her to Phuket and Bali, which was also enjoyable, more so as they were delighted by the little joys Niuniu experienced as she splashed around in the waves and tried to build sandcastles.

Once in a while, the thought of just selling their apartment and moving abroad does cross their minds. This is particularly so on days when the city is shrouded in smog, or another food contamination scandal is doing the rounds on WeChat, or worries of the future of the country or the intense competition that Niuniu will face in the *gaokao* (the university entrance exam) and myriad other fears about their lives are clouding their minds. But they shrug these off, feeling that they should just soldier on, as they have invested too much right here—not just financially, but also in relationships.

As they go about their daily lives, relishing its comfort and simple joys, they sometimes wonder about the big questions of life and the meaning of it all. But then these spiritual thoughts are pushed aside by day-to-day challenges and the joys of looking after their daughter. They wonder if they are bringing her up well and whether she will be able to have a secure and good life, and devote themselves to the daily business of remaining safe and healthy, and enjoying the comforts and indulgences that their parents never had access to, and that they never imagined that they themselves would benefit from.

On Average
Li Qiang and Wang Li are, of course, just one couple, but

they are broadly representative of their "young couples" group. For the purposes of this chapter, those young couples are defined as individuals born in the 1980s and 1990s (post-80s and post-90s, as they are referred to in China) who are married or are living together. Most of the post-80s would already be in a permanent relationship, whereas most of the post-90s, while perhaps not yet married, may already be in a serious relationship or living together. The average age of marriage in large cities like Shanghai is climbing and is nearly 33 years for men, and as high as 30 years for women—about ten years later compared to the early 1980s—although it is significantly lower for both in smaller cities. In fact, most Chinese feel that a woman should be married by about the age of 27, and unmarried women after the age of 30 or so are often disparagingly labeled as "left-over women." But again, this may be changing, especially in first-tier cities.

The average age of marriage has been creeping up for many reasons. Firstly, because of the historically strong parental preference for boys, there are around 20 to 30 million fewer women under 30 than men, which prolongs the search for a mate. Secondly, women are a bit better educated (52% of undergraduate and Master's degree students in Chinese universities are women) and more successful than men, and mostly want to "marry up," which narrows the field. Another factor is the increasing acceptance of pre-marital cohabitation—nearly 40% of married couples lived together before marriage, according to Zhenai.com, an online matchmaking service. However, unlike in some developed countries, cohabitation is in no way a substitute for marriage, but merely a delay. Unless unable to find a mate, most Chinese still prefer to "tie the knot," and face enormous social pressure to do so. Unfortunately this often leads to bad marriages and another modern phenomenon: rising divorce rates, which have increased by 63% in the past decade. In 2015, there were 2.79 divorces per 1,000 people, which is still far fewer than 16.9 in the United States.

The couples we concern ourselves with live in cities, where the most drastic social changes are happening, although many of them were born in rural areas. Like most everything else in China, the numbers involved are huge. Several factors will have a part in determining the size of this group in the coming years. Firstly, the tide of migration from countryside to cities, which has already resulted in over 250 million migrant workers, is likely to continue, but it is slowing. The World Bank estimated that increased productivity in agriculture will drive another 100 million rural residents to the cities in search of employment by 2030, which will bring China's urban population close to a billion.

The organic size of this segment in the cities may decrease over time and the population of singles may increase because of the paucity of women as well as over-ambitious demands and requirements from potential spouses. A Zhenai.com survey found that 34% of singles felt that they hold too high an expectation for a spouse, and nearly a quarter are willing to plod through life in a state of singlehood rather than compromise on their ideals, although it is unclear if they will actually do that. Lastly, that rising divorce rate will be a constraint.

The most peculiar demographic characteristic of young couples in China is that, at least in urban areas, both partners most often come from single-child families. As the "one child" policy was less rigorously enforced in rural areas, migrant couples in the cities sometimes have siblings. However, the majority of children born to young couples will never know an uncle or an aunt. Economically, it creates a relatively beneficial situation for them as they have few financial obligations with no siblings to look after, and parents who are normally at least able to look after themselves with their modest earnings or pensions, and who are very inclined to help their children out financially and contribute labor in the raising of a grandchild.

The parents of the young couples come from an era where urban housing was largely granted by the state, and hence they have no rent to pay, and if they were lucky and wise in trading and upgrading of property, could well be sitting on a pretty piece of real estate. In addition, the couples are the sole inheritors of their parents' wealth. The parents were not only able to afford to provide them with a good education, they are also able to give them a good start to their married life, including helping with the downpayment for a home, which in first-tier cities is incredibly expensive.

Diversity
Young urban couples in China are definitely not a single-target group with uniform behavior and preferences, but come in many colors and shades. Some variables on which they can be segmented are obvious: the city tier they live in, and whether they are local to the city (with the benefits of *hukou* registration that delivers access to healthcare and education) or have migrated from another place. Similarly, having or not having a child makes a big difference. And of course education and profession make huge differences to the kind of consumers they make.

While the internet has brought everyone closer together

and put everyone on an equal footing in terms of access to information and products, in has also tribalized young people by allowing them to pursue their own very individual interests in smaller, more connected groups, in ways not possible in the past. Brands would do well to recognize key tribes on the internet and attempt to develop a relationship with those with which they can interact meaningfully, as individuals naturally tend to remain in those tribes after marriage.

The city tier divide

China has around 650 cities (plus over 2,000 smaller towns), whose urban population ranges from over 20 million in Shanghai to less than a hundred thousand in small county-level cities. Like the rest of China's population, only a small minority of these couples live in the first-tier cities, with the largest proportion spread across over 250 prefecture-level cities. While efficient transportation links (including the high-speed rail network) and the reach of the internet have substantially reduced the differences between consumers living in large cities in relation to the smaller cities, the differences in lifestyle and mindset can be significant.

One key difference is employment opportunities and resulting incomes. Multinational companies and large well-paying private Chinese companies tend to be concentrated in the larger cities. The opportunity for livelihood in smaller cities is, therefore, mostly with the government or small private enterprises, which pay much less. Income in lower-tier cities is mainly from entrepreneurship, including moonlighting by underemployed workers in the public sector.

But despite this disparity, young couples in smaller cities have caught up with the larger-city residents in terms of consumption of basic products and services. According to data from Kantar Worldpanel, which measures household purchases of consumer goods, the lower-tier cities that were playing the catch-up game have now reached a similar level of saturation as the larger cities and are no longer able to provide volume growth to the most commonly used product categories.

The Average Age of First Marriage in the 20 Most Populous Countries		
Rank	Country	Average age at marriage
1	Germany	33.1
2	Brazil	30.8
3	Japan	30.5
4	United States	27.9
5	United Kingdom	27.9
6	Thailand	26.7
7	Turkey	26.2
8	Russia	25.7
9	Philippines	25.6
10	China	25.3
11	Iran	25.2
12	Nigeria	24.9
13	Egypt	24.8
14	Vietnam	24.6
15	Mexico	24.3
16	Ethiopia	23.5
17	DR Congo	23.4
18	India	22.8
19	Bangladesh	22.2
20	Indonesia	21.9

The average age of marriage in China is still below many Western nations, but it is rising
Source: Priceonomics

Young Couples and the Mobile Internet

The fact is that there are no young couples is China, only threesomes—the couple and the mobile internet. The post-90s generation have never seen a world without the internet, and the post-80s embraced the net at an early age and with unbridled enthusiasm. Young consumers (20-39 years old) constitute 54% of all internet users in China and are early adopters of the innovations and businesses developing around the internet. The internet in general and the mobile internet specifically has entirely transformed four key aspects of the consumers' lives: entertainment, information, shopping and social interaction.

Entertainment: Young couples' homes are quite likely to be adorned with a large LCD display (often more than one), but content consumption takes place far more on the tiny screen of their mobile phone. While the majority of consumers partake of free content, China in 2017 had 81 million paid online video service users subscribing to online platforms such as iQiyi, Tencent video and Youku.

Most importantly, the distinction between play time and work time has been blurred, as the two are often intermixed, and entertainment is consumed in small bites in between bouts of work. Entertainment has therefore been transformed from a discrete activity done in focused leisure to a near-continuous indulgence stolen in small pieces throughout the day.

Information: The conversion from discrete to continuous is true for other activities also. Young people do not wait for the newspaper to arrive every morning, but information rather continuously trickles to them through myriad online groups, websites, emails, newsletters and updates. As with people in many other parts of the world, young Chinese often imbibe more news from social networking websites than news channels.

Shopping: Shopping anywhere, anytime is the norm as technology places the world's supermarkets in the hands of Chinese consumers, with ordering and payments fast and convenient though the mobile phone. Though China is a distant second to the US in terms of the size of its consumer market, it is already the world's largest e-commerce market. According to the National Bureau of Statistics, China's online retail sales reached RMB 5.16 trillion ($752 billion) in 2016, up 26.2% over the previous year, which was still just 15.5% of the total RMB 33.23 trillion in sales. (The US, by contrast, grew its online retail by 15.6% to $394.86 billion in 2016, 11.7% of total retail sales.)

Social interaction: Because this generation grew up digital, it displays a closeness with the internet like no other generation (particularly the post-90s). Absence of siblings, aunts and uncles is all compensated by continuous interaction with a large number of friends and acquaintances on the internet. In fact, a common sight is a young couple having a meal together in a restaurant, each one absorbed in his or her own mobile phone, neglecting physical interaction for the sake of virtual companionship.

Lifestyle, Aspirations and Values

For young couples without a baby, the home is merely a place to sleep, with the focus of life, including nearly all meals, outside the house. This is despite the fact that home ownership is almost a pre-condition for getting married. In one survey in Shanghai, 70% of mothers of girls of marriageable age showed unwillingness to let their daughter marry a groom without an apartment. And although young couples almost always have help buying a home from their parents, it nevertheless places a huge financial burden on the couples, with many referring to themselves as *fang nu*, or house slaves, working only for the purpose of paying a mortgage.

A big differentiator in lifestyle is the type of city the couple resides in. For residents in lower-tier cities, the absence of a long commute provides more free time. As a result, traditional offline shopping and entertainment is more popular in smaller cities. Similarly, working for the government and smaller private companies, residents of lower-tier cities experience less competitive pressure than their counterparts in large companies in cities like Shanghai and Beijing. Most young couples living in lower-tier cities look up to the big cities, and yearn for the money and lifestyle that these cities provide, but they compromise to stay in their home cities for various reasons. (An emerging micro trend is couples from first-tier cities moving to lower-tier cities in search of a more relaxed lifestyle.)

Marketers often debate whether Chinese consumers in general, and particularly the relatively unique set of young consumers, have the same fundamental needs as consumers in the rest of the world. Needs are determined by a number of factors, and one of the more important determinants of needs are the basic values that we subscribe to. Values are all-encompassing beliefs that determine consumer lifestyle, behavior and preferences.

Numerous surveys have been conducted that measure Chinese consumers' values in comparison to the rest of the world (including the World Values Survey as well as periodic surveys by research organizations such as GfK and Illuminera). The most interesting aspect of the findings from these studies is that, in contrast to the common perception, the Chinese are not wired differently from those in the rest of the world. Just as people all over the world, the Chinese value family, honesty, friendship, self-reliance and open-mindedness. However, there are some differences, and in general the findings do support the popular belief that Chinese consumers place more emphasis on values such as duty, hard work and respect for elders. These values remain surprisingly consistent across different age groups. The key change is that duty and filial piety, though they remain important among the young, lose ground somewhat to the desire for learning and the search for fulfilling work, which have gained salience in this group.

Young Couples and Consumption

Although payments on the all-important house may eat into income a great deal, couples generally spend relatively little money there beyond the mortgage, particularly before the arrival of a baby. That means, of course, discretionary spending is largely done outside the home (again, until a baby comes along). There are several important trends to be aware of.

Premiumization: Young couples in urban China can swing from extreme price sensitivity to almost complete disregard of price. A vivid example of the latter is the way the preferred category for infant milk formula moved from low-priced local brands to very premium imported ones. Premiumization is key to the growth of many companies, as the market is becoming saturated. Data from Kantar Worldpanel shows that the categories benefitting most from premiumization in recent years have been foods such as yogurt and biscuits, skincare and make-up products and certain personal care products. On the other hand, consumers are not spending more on other products used in the confines of the home such as fabric care, toilet tissue and kitchen cleansers.

Consumption of services: One key aspect in which young couples differ from previous generations is higher consumption of services, including travel, hospitality, healthcare, entertainment and personal care.

The number of international tourists from China increased ten-fold from 2001 to 2015, with 122 million Chinese visiting an international destination in 2016. Some reports indicate that the Chinese already account for nearly a quarter of global outbound tourist consumption. It is not surprising, therefore, that hotels and tourist attractions all across the world are going an extra step to cater to Chinese tourists' tastes, including provision of an electric kettle in the room (hot water is a basic requirement for Chinese people, for drinking and for cooking instant noodles etc.) and bedroom slippers.

A brand which symbolizes the increasing acceptance of premiumization of services in China is Starbucks. Starbucks tends to maintain a near uniform pricing across all countries, and despite a per capita income one-tenth that of the United States, Starbucks sells its drinks at the same price in China as it does in the US. The key contributors to their success are the post-80s and post-90s sets, and their desire to indulge themselves not just by consuming an interesting product, but also enjoying the ambience, experience and modern, trendy image of the brand. Indeed, China has already become the second-most important market for Starbucks after the US.

Marketing to a Dynamic Generation

Young couples are possibly the most dynamic of the various segments of Chinese consumers, and their global exposure, as well as their internet and social media habits, ensure that they are always in tune with the rest of the world. At the same time, their relatively high levels of education, and ab-sence of traditional prejudices makes them extremely open to change and to embracing new ideas and services with eagerness.

Participants, not just recipients, of marketing messages: The older generations were content to sit in front of the TV and patiently absorb the messages thrown at them from brands. The digital world has changed this by transferring the control from marketer to consumer. Consumers today choose what content they consume and what ads they see, and most importantly what messages they share with oth-ers. Consumers now have a say in what messages are worth talking about and transmitting about a brand. In fact, the internet has been a boon for product enthusiasts who have access to all the information about a category or a brand, and may decide for themselves what is worth say-ing about a brand—and hence they are becoming creators of messages, in addition to being recipients. This has re-sulted in experienced and expert users turning into so-called "KOLs" (key opinion leaders) who not only transmit brand messages, but often also distribute the product. Marketers need to recruit the help from these KOL's to leverage their marketing efforts.

Shortening the consumer journey: Urban Chinese couples, particularly in the larger cities, are time poor. Long commutes, demanding work and overtime, exhausting entertainment, along with child care once a baby arrives leaves little time to pause and think about anything else, let alone brands. Marketers need to re-think their traditional strategies to reach the consumers in sequential, linear steps. Today's young consumers have minds of their own, and the confidence and impetuousness to try a brand as soon as they see it. Or on the other hand, they have the stubbornness to ignore repeated messages if a brand fails to resonate with them.

Increasing environmental consciousness: In most global surveys, Chinese consumers espouse strong environmental concerns and also demand responsible behavior from companies and from their government. The rare protests in China seem mostly to concern government projects which consumers see as harming their environment. The key question really is whether this conscienceness can translate into revenue and profits for marketers. In many areas it is already doing so. The key to selling green products to Chinese consumers is to link them to a core benefit which is of high value to them—protecting the health of their family. That of course will gain center stage as young couples, as they are prone to do, begin welcoming additions to the family.

Above all, understanding young Chinese couples is a good way to get a baseline on how much China has changed, and where things are going. While the younger generation will of course continue to evolve as they grow older, find partners and get married, this change will likely be more gradual, as opposed to the enormous, earth-shaking changes in China's recent past.

CHAPTER FOUR

Modern Chinese Mothers

Sizhang Kong

Part I: A Self-introduction

I was born in Inner Mongolia, and, like the subject of this chapter, I am a post-1980s mother who grew up in a relatively traditional society. Like more and more Chinese of the "New Middle Class," I have been lucky to have a global experience, living over the past 20 years in Beijing, Shanghai and Paris. I am also a consultant in a market research company where I lead research on family, modern Chinese mothers and their children.

For me, researching Chinese mothers is not only a business necessity, but also a personal desire. Especially with the arrival of my second son almost four years ago, I have realized how much I enjoy my role as a mother. I have also realized how important it is to understand myself and my role inside the family—the relationships between me and my mother, my husband and my two kids—and my place in wider society.

Over the hundreds of interviews that I have done with Chinese mothers in different Chinese cities, I have found that we have similar desires and anxieties. I am writing here about how I see the first generation of "modern mothers"—that is, those who have experienced the transformation of Chinese society from a highly traditional world that values self-sacrifice and obedience, to a world increasingly dominated by individualism (perhaps even hedonism), one in which women have begun to explore their deep desires, stand up for their rights and enjoy their liberties.

While this social change for Chinese women has been highly positive, it has also created unique difficulties. Particularly after motherhood, my generation of Chinese women experiences a painful tension, and sometimes daily conflict, between our inherited Chinese culture and newly-arrived Western values. Unsurprisingly, navigating personal and family issues has enormous impact on consumption as women define and then re-define who they are and who they want to be.

Part II: Meet Lily, In Two Different Worlds

Being a mother means to experience the tension between a modern Chinese woman's desire for liberty, indulgence and achievement, and her deeply-felt traditional duties in family and society. This tension, and the gap between one's life outside the home and inside the home, often creates the first major stress for a young mother in China today.

To fully illustrate this tension, I chose to tell the story of a Shanghai mother—Lily, we will call her—specifically because Shanghai is not a typical Chinese city. It is, arguably, the most competitive and individualistic city in China, and it is at the leading edge of modern development and culture. While Shanghainese women like Lily are perhaps not the most typical of Chinese women, their stories more clearly illustrate the conflict between Chinese and Western philosophy inside the family. Even in the most open-minded Chinese city, for China's most modern population, the domestic role for women is often still heavily emphasized.

Lily is a 33-year-old Shanghainese housewife. Her husband works as an engineer for a large Chinese IT company, earning about $4,000 per month, which is a solidly middle class salary for Shanghai. Lily describes him as a bit conservative, but very kind.

Before having her daughter, Duoduo, now four years old, Lily worked as assistant to the CEO of an American company. She enjoyed her career because she felt valued for her skill and competence. And because of the nature of her job, controlling the schedule of the CEO and managing complex office relationships, she had the satisfaction of exercising real power and responsibility.

The confidence it gave her was reflected in her social life. She stayed abreast of the trendiest topics in her circles, such as the goings-on in the world of high fashion, new product launches by the likes of Dior, and the opening of art exhibitions. It was the life that she imagined when she was in school, and she had put in many years of hard work to get it. She inhabited this life so fully as to develop the unconscious belief that it would never change.

Becoming a mother was a huge shock for her. Suddenly all her energy and income was spent on the baby—baby's clothes, baby's food, baby's toys. She began to forget her craving for Celine handbags, top-shelf makeup brands, and weekend shopping trips to Hong Kong with friends. She resigned from her job.

It also transformed her appearance. Lily remembers the first time she felt anxious in front of the mirror before taking her daughter out for a walk: unbranded athletic shoes, sportswear, no makeup, big backpack. She used to go out in her pumps and a short skirt, with only a handbag for her lipstick and mobile phone—now she looks like a "mom!"

She felt upset that she no longer looks so shining, a feeling surely almost any Western mother can understand. Feeling a bit upset at losing some of the brilliance of youth is perhaps a universal experience of motherhood. But for Lily it means the end of the modern life and a return, somewhat, to an older time—that of her own mother's—where women were expected to fit a more tightly-prescribed role in the family, mainly revolving around child care and little else.

Lily also felt a certain sense of danger for her family. She and her girlfriends often talked about their husbands, naturally, but after having children, anxiety began to sometimes creep into those conversations. As one friend warned: "If you don't take care of yourself, your looks, your hair, your husband will lose face. If you look completely like a mom from head to toe, your husband will leave you one day." Even if she does not believe that her husband would really leave her, it is an idea that sometimes gnaws at her.

At the same time, she also feels a disconnection from society. Before leaving her job, she often said to others, "you will become disconnected and marginalized if you don't work for a long time," and "a woman needs to work, otherwise you don't have respect." Now, of course, she has become that woman out of work—and she asks herself, "Where is my self-respect?" and "Where is my value?"

Partly because of this anxiety, Lily is actively searching for a flexible job that fits with her duties as a mother. She needs a job that will allow her to meet people, make personal connections, keep in touch with the world and, most of all, to make herself feel professionally and personally valued. She wants to find again that feeling of being a single woman: charming, social, independent and confident.

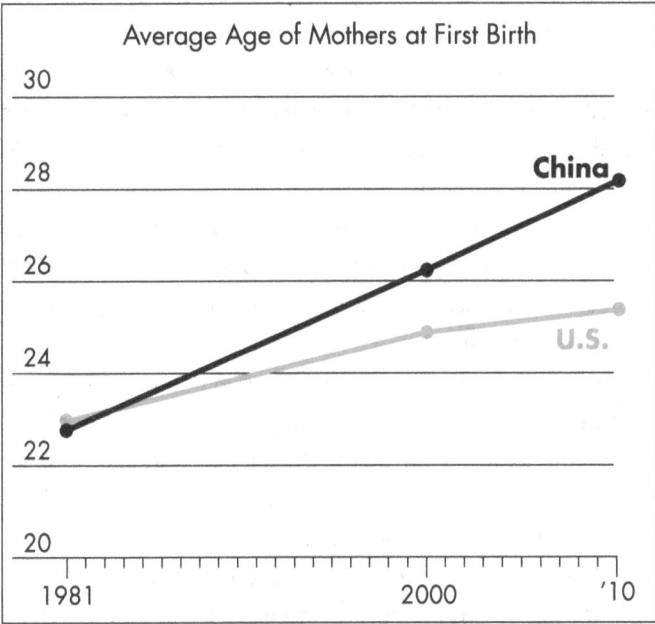

Average Age of Mothers at First Birth

The average age of first-time mothers has risen dramatically in China, a reflection of equally dramatic lifestyle changes
Source: The Wall Street Journal

Part III: Modern Mothers, Modern Families

If the desire to be a professional and brilliant woman in China remains somewhat limited to big cities like Shanghai, or to more open-minded women, the aspiration to become "modern mothers," with new, more Western attitudes toward parenting, education and nutrition, is prevalent across the entire country.

Thanks to her previous career, Lily knows many American families and she has always admired them: the kids almost invariably seemed healthy, beautiful and dynamic, and the mother always seemed to be able to handle several children as well as a career. She aspires to that image.

She's also rebellious toward her own upbringing. As a single child of a family of modest means, her parents did everything they could to provide for her, but she also resents that they were not able to simply spend more time with her—even today, they are not very close with her. Moreover, as is the case in traditional Chinese homes, her parents had a large degree of control over her life decisions: choice of university, choice of husband, choice of job—and if and when to leave it.

As a mother, she hopes to be more in line with her vision of Western parenting, giving liberty and respect to her kids, and being closer with them. Unlike her parents, who focused on education and material needs, she thinks that happiness is the most important element of a child's success.

Of course, these aspirations are often at odds with reality. For most young mothers, living up to these ideals is quite a bit harder than they can imagine, foremost because they still live in somewhat traditional homes. Particularly during a baby's first year, it is typical to have all four grandparents hovering about, which has a big influence on the home environment.

Like most other families of her generation, Lily delegates the baby's daily care to the grandparents. They come every day to prepare meals for her daughter and the family. After Duoduo was first born, she sometimes felt like she was barely a mother at all—she never even learned how to cook. Such as it is, young couples often feel it is nearly impossible to raise a child without relying on the grandparents.

The reasons behind this phenomenon are complex: in many cases, their own experiences as coddled only-children has resulted in a distinct lack of maturity in this generation of women that has left them unprepared for the challenging tasks of motherhood. This inexperience is reinforced by the fact that, again as the result of the one-child society, all four grandparents often have strong feelings of responsibility to aid in bringing up the grandchild.

Unsurprisingly, the grandparents running the show totally ignore the "modern parenting theories" that Lily has absorbed from books and the internet. They believe in their own experiences and adhere to the way they brought up kids 30 years ago. The result is a constant struggle in every aspect of childcare from food, to activities, and even to bathing.

For mothers like Lily, this situation can be exhausting, but on the other hand it is tough to imagine getting on without the help of the grandparents, at least before the child goes off to kindergarten.

On the edge of this intergenerational struggle is the issue of fatherhood. In Chinese families, the father can still often be somewhat absent from domestic life because the social role of the father is directed mainly toward the outside world.

Lily's husband is often considered to be a model man by friends and family. He has a good salary; he gives all he earns to his wife; he doesn't cheat on her; he drives their daughter to pre-school and to the doctor. From the traditional viewpoint, what else is there to desire in the father of your child?

But, for Lily, it doesn't match the image of happy modern

couple and family that she absorbed from the internet and social media, which advocate more communication, equality and respect in a marriage. Her husband lacks a certain degree of involvement with the family. She wishes her husband spent more time with their daughter and with her. She wishes he could be more active in organizing family activities and vacations, and also in managing the house. Lily does all these things, seemingly with little appreciation.

The overwhelming popularity of the reality TV show *Baba Qu Nar?* (roughly translated as *Where are We Going, Dad?*) is a good reflection of the common lack of parenting by fathers in China. The show depicts male Chinese celebrities traveling to places in rural China alone with their kids. It shows how father and child overcome difficulties together. This show, now in its fifth season, attracts some 75 million viewers each episode, and has provoked heated discussion about the place of the father inside the family, and why fathers are often not so emotionally involved with their children.

Lily herself is an avid fan, and gets involved actively in the discussion, often sharing articles with her husband and friends. The topic of conversation with her girlfriends is often about how to get their husbands to spend more time and energy on the family. On the whole, Lily is fighting against a traditional family model that values more the practical organization of family than sincere and emotional relationships between family members.

Faced with such difficult challenges in so many aspects of family life, young mothers across China have come to rely heavily on social media for information and support.

Lily is in at least ten WeChat groups for mothers, each

focusing on different topics such as education, child nutrition, English reading and so on. In addition to these, she follows a dozen or so WeChat public accounts (akin to blogs) of parenting experts.

This digital and horizontal support plays a huge role in her life. Information about new ideas and products is quickly spread through these digital platforms: learning groups around new topics such as "positive discipline," "how to educate kids without yelling," and "how to be a better mother," can easily gather thousands of mothers in several hours.

Part IV: Consumption

For Lily, as for other mothers in China, consumption of new products is one way of challenging tradition in their everyday lives, and also a way of constructing new habits, consistent with their image of modern mothers. The right products can be powerful tools for them in their transformation, and also serve as labels of their status as part of the "New Middle Class." They can also allow mothers to introduce new daily rituals without provoking conflict with grandparents, and to please children without losing control.

The most important characteristic of a Chinese mother's consumption as related to the child is that it often goes together with a learning process. Mothers begin to collect information as soon as they are pregnant: from knowledge about nutrition to products suitable for a house with a baby. For some, this search can result in complete changes of thinking and behavior. In a short period, they become equipped with mountains of knowledge and also, naturally, brand impressions that help build their aspirational image of parenthood and family.

On the other hand, the level of concern felt by mothers can mean that purchasing decisions can become quite a laborious process. Lily spent more than two months doing research before deciding to buy Aptamil baby formula for her daughter. She visited dozens of websites, compared comments from existing users as well as experts. In the process, she became quite familiar with all the nutrition that a baby needs.

Following that, she spent perhaps even more energy debating with the grandparents, who preferred the competing brand Illuma. Her parents were more attracted by Illuma's bold, aspirational advertising promising ambitious and intelligent children. But she persisted in her own selection, which was informed by her online community of mothers—Aptamil, they told her, is the closest to breast milk.

In addition to nutrition, another common topic of obsession has been early childhood reading. Lily bought her daughter many imported books, which are filled with beautiful, imaginative illustrations. By contrast, she tends against Chinese storybooks, which are often "morality-oriented"—perhaps evidence of her desire to foremost giver her daughter happiness.

When it comes to clothing, Lily has a big budget to buy the best. She wants to make her daughter into a beautiful princess and instill in her a good sense of taste as early as she can. She is not satisfied with the grandparents who don't understand fashion and often mix and match clothes randomly. Of course, she will never directly point that out to her parents—she often simply hides the old-fashioned clothes bought by grandma.

That kind of conflict avoidance is a strategy pursued by

many young mothers in China when dealing with grandparents. They adhere to tradition: being respectful, caring for their health, buying them expensive nutritional supplements. And when it comes to disagreements, they can be more passive: ignoring negative comments on clothing or lifestyle, sticking the ugly clothes in the back of the drawer, and venting to other mothers on social media. It preserves a sense of harmony.

Lily's spending is often organized around her daughter, but extends beyond her. Lily, daughter and husband often spend their weekends together in big shopping malls that offer educational classes for kids such as English and painting, but also entertainments for adults and fashionable restaurants. It is a popular way for mothers to combine parenting time and relaxation time.

The kitchen is another place of transformation. Lily's kitchen has changed a lot since she has settled into motherhood. "Healthy" has become a key word in her life. She not only finally learned to cook, but has equipped her kitchen with all of the best machines: a blender, a juicer, a yoghurt maker and a better oven.

Since the arrival of Duoduo, Lily does not go out to restaurants or take delivery food as often as before, as she perceives both to be less than healthy. Neither does she want her parents to always cook their oily traditional food, which also often smokes up the house. Instead, her new tools help her to fulfill her new requirements for food: healthy, easy to prepare, and of course aesthetically pleasing. Her new sensibilities naturally extend to ingredients as well. Her fridge is stocked with new and imported items: butter, cream, tomato sauce, Italian pasta, cheese, steak and salmon.

In short, consumption has played a huge role in Lily beginning to live out her ideal of becoming a "modern mother." However, that has also come together with new financial pressure. Owning a car, traveling, buying international brand goods for Duoduo, paying for pre-school and extra classes and so on has become the standard for "new middle class" families—and it is not cheap. Just a pair of shoes can cost over $50, pre-school can be $30 an hour. It sometimes seems that to remain a part of this new middle class, Lily and her husband have to spend all their money. Although $4,000 a month is already a good salary, they still don't feel very secure. They are afraid of unexpected unemployment, significant illness, and the thought of having a second child makes them feel anxious.

But the social pressure is more often than not greater than the financial pressure. Lily in fact thinks that maybe pre-school is not necessary, but when all the other parents send their children there, Lily doesn't want to be excluded. After all, what parent doesn't want to provide a good future for their child? The pre-school looks wonderful with beautiful classes, native-English-speaking teachers and a happiness-oriented mentality. Lily is convinced that it represents the most up-to-date ideas about education.

Lily also tries to spend a bit on herself: beauty remains a necessity for modern women, including mothers. It gives her confidence and it constructs a visible differentiation compared to her own mother. Buying an annual gym membership is also a necessity—whether or not she goes is second to the fact of merely possessing it, because she can use it to prove her commitment to "modern" attitudes about health.

Generally speaking, Lily feels better with all these new

items (though she acknowledges the negatives of material-ism, including cost). They allow her to progressively build up her new life as a mother having real value and pleasure inside the house. Motherhood for her is not a role of sacri-fice, but a real motor of transformation, of creativity and of positivity for the whole family. It is not a passive role, but an active position that binds the family together.

One day, when I asked her to reflect on her thus-far four years of experience as a mother, her answer surprised me: "Painful, but happy because I've 'grown up' together with my daughter. I couldn't imagine all that I can do before hav-ing my daughter. I'm stronger than I thought!"

Part V: Conclusion

Looking at the story of Lily is to look at my own experience in the mirror. With the arrival of my second son, I have un-derstood how a child can be a real booster for his mother, instead of a handicap. And, like Lily, I have come to have a greater sense of fulfillment in life.

Many young mothers in China are still struggling with the sometimes opposing ideals of being a modern woman and being a mom. But the strength of the post-80s mothers is in their motivation, positivity and flexibility to be involved in the transformation of society by creating a better life for themselves and their families.

Today, consumption and digital community mean em-powerment and openness for these young mothers. Chil-dren are the place of transformation and revolution for these young mothers today, because they need to discover their own value by gaining control of their own lives, and constructing their own place in the family without provoking too much conflict.

CHAPTER FIVE

Successful Single Women

Annie Fang

THE ROLE OF women in Chinese society has been changing with a speed and intensity to match the vast economic changes that have occurred since the 1970s, and what is considered to be "success" for a woman in China has changed dramatically. The simple ideal of marrying into a good family is, at least in China's first-tier cities, a thing of the past, even to the point where "housewives" may be somewhat looked down upon. Replacing it is a mixture of modern ideals involving education, career, wealth and family.

But while few in either China or the West would argue against an expanded role and higher expectations for women in modern China, the exact mixture of personal goals and family responsibilities, individual ambition and social conformity, is a source of tension. For no group is this truer than China's "Successful Single Women," or those who have made it in the professional world while remaining unmarried into their late 30s and 40s.

The character Andy in the TV series "Ode to Joy," a drama centering on five different women living in the same apartment building in Shanghai, is a reflection of the successful woman's uncertain and evolving position in modern China. A former Wall Street executive, Andy would have been considered a "monster career woman" (女强人) five years ago, but is now the idol of girls at the entry level. The popularity of the TV series has brought about booming sales of clothes on Taobao marketed as "Andy Style" (安迪同款). Money, status and experience—Chinese women are finding the courage to ask for more of both the world and of themselves.

Yet how much independence is "appropriate" for a woman? Independent women themselves cannot fully agree on this. Although money, status and experience can be admired, can one's status of "single" be fully accepted? Can single women fully embrace who they are? These are difficult questions for both individual women, and for Chinese society as a whole.

This chapter focuses on the struggle to answer these questions for this unique group of Chinese women who have been able to grasp the opportunities of modernity while still feeling the pressures of traditional society. And though they may not always be able to arrive at satisfying conclusions, they absolutely don't want to be handed the answers.

Modern China, Modern Opportunity
Traditional Chinese culture, very roughly speaking, de-emphasizes individuality, and instead emphasizes submissiveness, obedience and the fulfillment of duties. While these cultural prescriptions have held for both genders, as China was traditionally a highly patriarchal society, they were tougher on women. It didn't matter who you were as a woman, but rather how you fulfilled your duties as a mother, daughter and wife. Meaning in life was derived almost solely from being part of something, namely the family.

The forces of modernization have greatly tempered this

traditional perspective on life. The One-Child Policy, although far from being all positive in its impact, has helped give women the chance to be considered as important as men, particularly in big cities with educated populations, as parents can have only one child to love and cherish. Explicit state efforts at enforcing gender equality, although far from perfect, have also had positive effects—public education and university, for example, has tended away from gender bias in modern China. That has laid down the foundation for women to compete on comparatively fair grounds with men starting from an early stage in life.

China's booming economy also brought with it chances for women to move up, both in the generation of jobs and in the introduction of fresh ideas from abroad. The 1990s was a boom era for multinationals entering China, and the largely performance-based company cultures created attractive opportunities for hard-working women to pursue careers. State-owned companies, by contrast, were still deeply mired in the traditional mindset that women needed to be more devoted to the family. Managers would worry, "Will she get pregnant right after I hire her?"

More recently, the call for innovation and entrepreneurship by the government has been re-setting the scene once again. People are asked to think and act in different ways, where the hottest words these days are "disruption," "upgrading" and "innovation."

Chinese women have heeded this call in a big way. As the *Bloomberg* news service noted in 2016, Chinese women have broken the glass ceiling in the world of venture capital: "Among the top US venture firms, women make up about 10% of the investing partners and only half of the firms have any women of that rank. China is already more balanced: About 17% of investing partners are female and 80% have at least one woman." Indeed, the biggest VC fund ever raised by a woman is in China.

Pressures, Old and New

As these new opportunities have emerged, relationships have changed, and so have the pressures that go along with them. There are parents above, romantic/marital interests in the middle, and a sharp and competitive layer of youth below.

Parents: "Filial piety," or duty towards one's parents, is among China's most deeply-rooted values. In basic terms, it involves obedience to and sacrifice on behalf of parents, and traditionally gives parents a high degree of control over the lives of their children, particularly daughters, including decisions about marriage. For many successful women, financial independence and fresh experience has wrought a new view of the world that does not involve blind obedience. *"I can respect you, provide you with sufficient money and care, yet I cannot let you dictate my life."* Given the expectations, it is not an easy attitude to adopt—for many women, setting down the limits also entails guilt and conflict. Before, a daughter was expected to do what was "right," to settle down, to bring forth grandchildren. For the older generation of parents, missing this obligation is often not taken lightly, modern life or not.

Lovers: If a single word can describe these women, it is "competitive." They don't want to lose to anyone in any field, including dating, and they demand equal footing in any relationship. Many Chinese men feel threatened by this "fierce" attitude. Some of these women in big cities tend to have more dating experience with foreigners than locals. When there are provocative reports about Chinese girls marrying foreigners for a US or European visa, they shake their heads: "I am making no less, maybe even more, than my foreign boyfriend." It goes without saying that these single women can never accept the type of married life their parents have, simply "getting by" (过日子), having fierce fights but never getting a divorce. In their eyes, miserable marriages were the norm because in the past the only thing that mattered was getting married, more often than not as young as possible. And yet many times, these successful single women do not have the capacity to deliver on the type of love and relationship they aspire to. Their parents haven't shown them and school hasn't taught them. It takes time and effort to build a loving relationship, but they spend more time in the office than at home. Aggressiveness can win in a career, but in a relationship, one needs to compromise. At the same time, their standards for men tend to be extremely high, as they prefer to "marry up."

Subordinates: These women meet their younger counterparts, the "post-90s," in the office with a mixture of awe and respect. They find ways to connect while still keeping a distance to ensure their authority. They know clearly that this is an era where the older generation needs to learn from the younger. The accumulated insights and professional knowledge possessed by these single women are now being taught in school, leaving a slimmer knowledge gap—and what's more, younger colleagues often have better command of things like social media. Though it is tough for them to admit it, as the desire to stay in control and maintain authority is strong, they need to learn from the younger group. Yet secretly they are picking things up, even trivial things, like learning to accept the fact that work is moving more and more off email and onto WeChat. At the end of the day, they are afraid of being overtaken.

The Lives of Two Women

With these realities and forces in mind, let us take a look at the life stories of two successful single Chinese women.

Angela: From Childhood to Career

Angela is a more or less typical "post-80s" woman, born into an average family in Shanghai where both parents were factory workers. The whole family had been expecting a baby boy, and thus had not prepared a proper name for a girl. When they reported her birth with the local authorities, her rushed parents registered her name as simply "Sister," which she officially kept until reaching school age.

As obedient citizens who valued stability above all, Angela's parents complied with the one-child rule, despite yearning for a second child. And so, like most of her generation, Angela became the sole carrier of all the hopes and dreams of her family, the expectations of which only grew with the widening income gap generated by China's newly liberalizing economy.

Her childhood years were filled with extra-curricular lessons, and intense pressure to succeed. She remembers gatherings of the wider family centering on discreet rivalry among the adults, who would compete in humble-bragging about their children. Such was the value and focus on children in working-class families without much other success.

Angela's early school life could be considered a text-book case for what a good Chinese student was supposed to be. She was obedient to her parents, and a top-three student in the eyes of her teachers. She accepted all the standards put forward for her without questioning her reality one bit.

As a teenager in high school, where dating and romance were banned, she found she had a rebellious streak and got herself her first boyfriend. "When I look back at my life, I realize it is more accurate to say I did that to make my parents unhappy, rather than falling for the boy," she says today.

It did make them unhappy. Angela was quickly disciplined and she returned to her normal quiet, obedient self, carrying the "future hopes" of the family. It was a mission she eventually fulfilled, as she went on to rank among the top students in high school, attend a good college, and after graduation land a job at an international consulting firm.

The first few years of her career life in the world of multinationals was akin to progressing through a video game—level by level, with each completed challenge being followed by a harder one.

"Every day you are trying to beat the monster," Angela says.

At the same time, she feels lucky to have been able to work in such a mature company, one that was both organized and that also rewarded hard work and ambition with regular promotions. There is, however, a familiar pressure about such a system where the standard benchmarks are set, and age-vs-title is the indicator of success. The constant comparisons to others was not unlike school as a child.

"You cannot help but be a bit obsessed about the age of your peers at the same level," she says. "Should he or she be younger than you, a sense of jealousy rises up from your stomach, even if it is only one year difference. You constantly check how your former classmates are doing. Are they making more or less money than you? Are they advancing faster or slower than you?"

The workload was heavy and the traveling relentless. Angela cannot remember how many times she has taken the last flight to another city before getting up at 6am for a 7am meeting. Sometimes she felt there was nothing good about working in an international firm, but she cannot deny that the organization seemed to care little about gender.

"What your boss cares about most is your deliverables," she says. "This is what 'equality' means."

Angela advanced quickly in her management consulting career, but before she knew it, the changing economy saw the "dream consulting firms" turning into "conventional industry."

After companies like Tencent and Alibaba started doing IPOs, Angela began to have a growing sense of urgency about the changing world. Fewer people seemed to admire her job in an international consulting firm, and the younger generation embraced a new ideology, the "Internet mindset" (互联网思维) of moving first and adjusting later, rather than making meticulous calculations.

Faced with a changing reality, a sense of anxiety overwhelmed her. A voice in her head warned she would lose her job and her glory someday if she didn't make a change.

At age 34, Angela left the firm and ventured into the startup field. Although she doesn't know where this new track will lead her to, she feels clearly that the old path clearly led in the direction of career death.

Daughter — Lover
Angela's success and ambition as a professional woman has had a big, and sometimes unexpected, impact on many aspects of her personal life.

Starting when she was about 30, conflict began to grow between her and her parents, whose pressure on her was unending.

"They do not demand anything from themselves, and yet they demand a million things from me," she says. "They are only satisfied when I am the top achiever, yet they don't spare any effort to improve themselves, not picking up a book to read, not taking up a new course to polish their skills."

She has mostly kept this resentment to herself, along with a bit of guilt about it. But the release of the best-selling 2016 book, *The Giant Baby Nation* (巨婴国), by a Chinese psychologist, helped her bring these issues out in the open. She cannot agree more with the central points of the book—that traditional Chinese parents force their children to "merge" with themselves so that they can carry out the dreams they themselves cannot realize—and it impacts on mental maturity. What is more insidious is that the bad cultural habits are subtly packaged under the idea of "filial piety" (*Xiao* 孝). This book helped Angela get past some of her anxieties.

As for relationships, Angela has dated more foreigners than local Chinese. She has particularly cherished the romantic freedom she experienced when on long-term work stays overseas. Abroad, her status as a "left-over woman" (unmarried and over 30) disappeared, and women of her personality and position turned out to be popular and attractive. It makes her feel better about not being "docile and obedient."

"Sexy—if you ask me, I would say Miranda in *Sex and the City* defines the new sexy," she says. "It's about the courage you have."

Angela grew up watching Hollywood movies, and that informed her relationship ideals—a perfect connection between a couple—even though she herself is not aware of it.

However, while she says that men and women are equal, a man less successful than her can never impress her. A name card emblazoned with the title VP or CEO impresses her, even though she herself doesn't realize that the attraction is closely bound to her own career aspirations.

Luck finds her in love with a foreign guy who is willing to move back to China with her. Yet by the time they truly start a relationship in the same city, reality kicks in, and whenever she faces a conflict between work and the relationship, work is always the priority. The fire gradually died down, even though she herself was not aware of the cause.

After a rough breakup, she picked herself up by voraciously reading articles related to human psychology, just like any other well-educated professional woman would do. It dawned on her that the capacity she has to sustain and nurture a relationship is not sufficient to deliver the quality of love to which she aspires.

The concept of love in a traditional Chinese family amounts to simply "co-existence." Authority and duty outweighs empathy and communication. Sustaining something more than that requires time and effort—and she is determined now to learn the right skills to make love work.

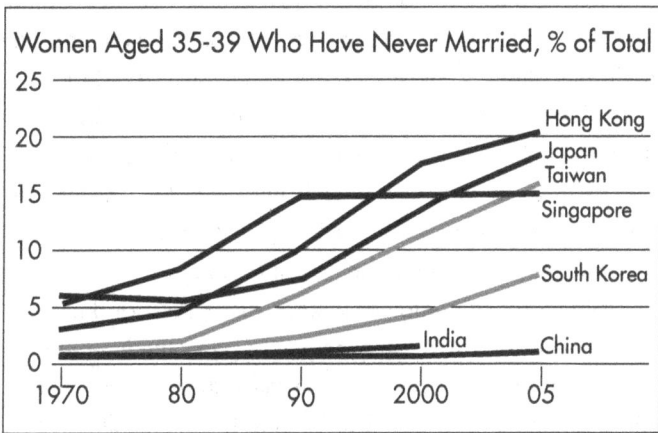

Women Aged 35-39 Who Have Never Married, % of Total

The number of women who never marry in China is low,
both absolutely and comparatively. But this group is culturally
important and growing
Source: The Economist

Cathy in the Big City

Unlike Angela, Cathy was born in a small village. When she landed in the world, there was not much celebration, but much determination on the part of her parents to get pregnant again so that they could have a boy.

A few years later they succeeded, and the new baby boy made her invisible. No matter how hard she tried and how good her performance was at school, she failed to get attention from her parents. Even the better food, whatever eggs and meat that could be had in the village, was mostly reserved for her brother.

Starting from an early age, she whispered a little secret to herself, "I will leave this place one day." The one and only way to achieve that was to study hard and get into college in a big city.

Cathy achieved that goal, getting into Central China Normal University, in Wuhan, but her admission brought the family little joy. Her mom had hoped she would take up a job after finishing high school, "to help the family financially, just like what the neighbors' daughters are doing." Her mom even teamed up with her other relatives to try talking her out of attending college, but Cathy resisted hard until her parents had no choice but to relent.

Cathy took up computer science as a major and marketing as a minor, as computer science signals the future while marketing was considered to be the hottest job a multinational could offer in the 2000s. She finished college with the help of student grants and money from part-time jobs.

Partly because of her humble background, Cathy always tried to put forward her best, no matter if it was in academic work or the way she dressed—she had to be better than the rest, or at the very least no worse.

Four years of hard work at school and internships during breaks earned Cathy a secure place in the job market in Beijing, and yet there was still some way to go to make it to her dream job at a multinational—locals raised in the urban environment had a leg up on her. But eight years of a workaholic lifestyle at a local firm finally earned her an offer into the marketing department of a multinational.

Cathy's circle of friends in the city slowly expanded as well, which was also a goal she aspired to, although she could be a bit timid socially. While gradually adapting to the patterns of urban life, her old life in the countryside became more distant. Yes, she missed her mom from time to time when things got tough in her new life. But spending time with family members in the village during Chinese New Year become more difficult with each passing year. She tried everything to avoid the "kind" warnings from everyone that "it's better for women to get married early."

Growing Older
Cathy only feels comfortable when she is the best. She needs to stand out in every aspect in front of her friends, and that of course includes the realm of boyfriends. When she started dating a pilot with a foreign airline, she made sure that everyone around her knew about it, as if she had won herself a trophy. But the relationship did not last long.

Similarly, Cathy was not long with her coveted multinational firm before MNCs were no longer considered to be the apex of success. Society had shifted its attention towards the startup scene and the venture capital community—her ambition followed suit. She tendered her resignation and signed herself up for an investment course in the UK, which cost her 30% of her savings. Coming back to China with the plan of setting up a mutual fund, she faced doubt from everyone around her, especially from men. *"It is better for a woman to work in a mutual fund than to set up her own firm. Starting from scratch with such a thing is just crazy."*

In many ways, it was actually crazy. Anxiety over her ventures delivered her many sleepless nights, yet her inner voice drove her to prove herself, on her own, with no help.

Her pursuit of perfection is deeply personal. Whenever she meets up with her girlfriends, it is important to subtly pass on the message that there is a constant stream of men chasing after her: "I had this guy 'bugging' me asking me out, but I'm not quite sure if I like him." Her girlfriends, knowing what she wants, respond with expressions of awe, eyes wide open: "Wow, you are so popular!"

Her ambition in appearance is as big as her ambitions in love and career. Cathy always makes sure she is immaculately made-up and dressed. She wraps herself in floor-sweeping skirts, of which she has more than 50. "This is me, never a repeated look in a month."

Cathy may not be totally satisfied with her life, but she wouldn't trade it for anything.

Uncertainty – Branding

Anxiety is a theme in the lives of China's successful single women, no matter how impressive their past achievements. The stable fast-track career path is disappearing. Multinationals have given way to startups. And, as people inevitably do, they are getting older, and in a culture that still prizes family.

The key words of this market segment are change/uncertainty (混沌). Those who stay as the top management in big firms fear they are aging out of competitive professions. When the article "Where do marketing directors go after 40 years old?" was published on WeChat in August, 2017, it got over ten thousand hits in one day. The author tapped into the anxiety people feel about getting older and slowing down in the face of fresh blood coming out of school, and losing a certain personal grip on things. "Will the experiences I have accumulated over the years become obsolete over night?" Cathy asked.

Those who have already ventured into entrepreneurship are putting out their best to deal with real ambiguity and uncertainty for the first time in their lives.

Reaching Single Women

Brands in the China market need to be aware of the fact that it is no longer a question of whether Chinese women should be independent or not, but a matter of to what degree and at what speed. They are like rubber bands being stretched to different lengths at different speeds. They may be originally from the same place, but they slowly drift apart into separate camps. Speaking to them is therefore difficult, a matter of subtlety. It may be easier to look at examples of what does and doesn't work.

In 2016, cosmetics brand SKII drew international praise for a marketing project staged in People's Square Park in Shanghai, which famously hosts a roughly weekly local "marriage market" where the parents of unwed Chinese come to play matchmaker (notably without the matches present). In the ad, single women whose parents have taken to the market confront their parents with their true anxieties over the issue in emotional on-camera encounters.

The ad had a certain power, but for many successful single women, it was a turn off. The SKII piece won the hearts of those women who have already somewhat resigned themselves to the traditional role, but it upset successful single women who are determined to make their own way.

This desire for "independence with family consent" may resonate well with a less determined, less adept audience, but the successful singles are used to giving the world a hard stare. Grayness and gloom, sadness and pity, as well as reminders of the obligation to family harmony—these are the last things this group wants to see.

Successful single women want the fun they have and their exciting lifestyles to be seen. They want their courage in adversity to be admired, and their exploration of life's possibilities to be encouraged. They will never surrender to a list of responsibilities they need to have only because they are women.

They may have hard times where they have to pull themselves and be strong despite deeply felt vulnerability. But their acceptance of their vulnerabilities is what gives them courage. This is exactly what makes the recent Lancôme campaign, "My Vulnerability Is My Strength" (我的脆弱就是我的强大), work so well.

In the ad, Lancôme uses the heroine Tang Jing from the TV serial My First Half of Life, who represents a typical successful single woman—hard-working, taking one's job as the foundation of independence, tough and never giving in to the male partner in competition. The role has been criticized by some as tough on the outside but weak inside. Yet this is exactly the vulnerable moment where courage is seen.

For brands that hope to embrace the idea of independence to connect with this audience, it is critical to scrutinize the message you want to send out, as the lullaby for some could be bothersome noise for others.

CHAPTER SIX

The Freshly Graduated

Francesca Hansstein

YOUNG AND INTELLECTUAL, oversized round glasses. Fitted cap and pre-ripped jeans. Afternoon patio latte selfie, a skateboard as a fashion statement. Open to changing jobs, jumps the internet firewall every day. Has an opinion, understands subtle use of emojis. Culturally aware, consciously delaying marriage. Sure of who they are, but not of what they want.

These young adults, just graduated from prestigious Chinese colleges, put a high premium on meaningful pursuits. For their parents' generation, career is chiefly practical—a calculation of stability and earning potential, a return on investment. But young graduates in China are generally not interested in an "iron rice bowl," and the steady thrum of 9-to-5 seems not to promise fulfillment; instead, it drives them to search.

Often referred to (somewhat derisively) as the "post-90s generation," they are regarded by their elders as infamously unsettled, taken to switching jobs, or even making major career turns, seemingly at the drop of a hat. Characteristically they set out for something more creative: jumping from office to business startup, from math to fashion, from accounting to journalism.

But it would be a mistake to think they are simply blowing in the wind. These youngsters are engineers when it comes to building social ties and adjusting their lives. They know that they are in China and that here more than anywhere else, *guanxi*—one's web of personal and professional relationships—is paramount for career advancement.

More often than not, their English is good, as is their understanding of Western culture. Their identities are well defined—they know who they are, and are less inclined to let institutions or traditions decide for them.

The young generation has strong preferences for quality over quantity. This is reflected in their taste and by the brands they chose—organic food, Korean make-up, European fashion, and so on—through which they proudly signal their educated social status. They are not rich, but they are also not worried.

These new young, urban, brand-conscious, health-oriented, smart, critically-thinking budding professionals are, to borrow the Western characterization, China's emerging "yuppies."

To get a handle on them for this chapter, a total of 35 in-depth interviews were conducted to shed light on their characteristics, preferences and lifestyles. Interviews targeted young adults between 23 and 28 years of age who graduated at most five years ago from universities in first and second-tier cities. The vast majority reported to be financially independent after about one year after graduation, were satisfied with their job, and optimistic about the future. Many of them still live with their parents or relatives (if in the same city) or share an apartment with roommates, especially when they live in metropolitan areas, like Shanghai, where housing price have soared in the last few years.

Age of Plenty

In the last ten years, the number of young adults graduating from Chinese universities has mushroomed. While those nearest to the top of the heap can get educated overseas, the great majority earn their diplomas domestically (about 98%). According to China's Ministry of Human Resources and Social Security, China expects 8.2 million new college graudates in 2018, ten times as many as in 1997. In other words, this is first generation in China with truly mass higher education.

Chinese parents, being the practical people that they are, and with the education system in China being focused more on rote learning, often favor majors in hard skills such as information technology and engineering. However, there is a growing interest in humanities, although official figures are hard to come by.

The quality of education in China has significantly improved in the last few decades, and it is not rare to spot Chinese Universities among the top positions of world university rankings. *Times Higher Education* ranks Peking University and Tsinghua University (comparable to Ivy League schools in terms of domestic prestige) in the top 50 institutions worldwide. Certain subjects perform even better—in the *U.S. News and World Report's* 2017 ranking for Best Global Universities for Engineering, Tsinghua University beat MIT for the top spot, and four of the top ten were Chinese.

As the quality of these institutions has improved (along with the growth of the economy in China), the character of graduates has evolved. According to MyCOS, a higher education research firm, in recent years about one-in-eight young graduates wants to be their own boss. Rather than accepting the rules of a workplace, these young professionals would rather go the extra mile to earn their freedom. Indeed, in 2015, an average of 12,000 companies were registered in China every single day.

Many of this educated hip set choose to make a go of it in businesses that cater principally to their own demographic—such as starting a small café with a limited, but carefully curated, menu, or a clothing boutique. Shanghai's central Jing'an District has become of hive of such small business activity, where they dominate the blocks within eyesight of stores like Gucci and Prada.

Not everyone has the resources—or the bravery—to open up their own company, but the mindset of taking control of one's life extends well into less entrepreneurial career paths. It is increasingly common to find young people who are willing to make daring career moves. In some cases, they simply want to try something more exciting.

Another aspect worth mentioning is the role of *guanxi*, the system of social relationships that creates important advantages, including kicking-off a career. This is particularly true in a fiercely competitive environment, and if some fresh graduates complain about the relative unfairness embedded in this system (*"unfair social competition"* was often mentioned in the survey), most invest a significant amount of their time in building out their strategic personal connections.

Save It... or Spend It?

Just as the views on career for this group differ from older generations, so do its views on consumption.

The older generation in China is famously frugal. In 2013, China's gross savings as a percentage of GDP was just a shade below 50%, and third highest in the world behind small Kuwait and tiny Bermuda, according to data from the World Bank. The United States, by comparison, was only 18%. China's sky-high savings rate has helped fuel the country's rise, as the banks were able to put that money to work investing in infrastructure and the like.

The younger generation, while perhaps not as profligate as their counterparts in US, live life much differently from their parents. They face a dilemma between saving up for big-ticket purchases such as housing and cars, both of which are extremely expensive relative to incomes in China and culturally very important, and the desire to embrace a rising consumer culture and enjoy life, which of course means spending for today.

With the rise of e-commerce, that spending has become easier than ever. The absolute number of online shoppers has been steadily increasing in China since 2006, reaching 467 million in 2016. According to official data, in 2015 the 20-29 generation represented 31% of all online buyers, followed by the 10-19 and the 30-39 age groups with shares of 24.5% and 23.5% respectively. The young generation is also more sophisticated in its consumption habits. They are much more likely to be experienced overseas travelers, brand-conscious and skilled digital consumers, all aspects that make their tastes worldly and well-defined. Online giants Alibaba and JD.com occupy more than 75% marketshare in e-commerce, although smaller niche players are growing, particularly in higher-quality goods. Those below 28 years old represent 40% of shoppers on Taobao, owned by Alibaba, and concentrate their shopping in the evening hours.

But while this group is spending more, their parents have at least passed on some habits—their appetite for deals, discounts and promotions, for instance, is insatiable. Popular apps like Meituan specialize in group-buying, a Groupon-like model that ensures a discount only after a certain number of customers have pledged to buy, which young people use to screen for the ultimate online deals.

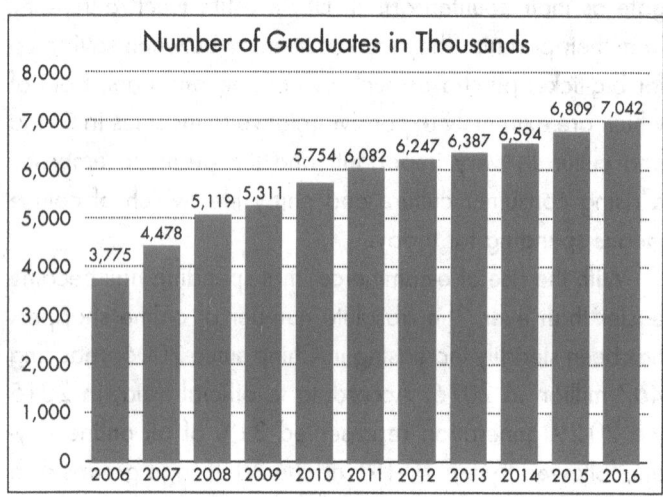

The rising number of university graduates in China is changing both the job market and the culture of young people
Source: Statista

Refining Taste

In getting to know these fresh young faces, it is helpful to understand what they buy in various segments. In terms of consumption within this group, three big areas are key to understanding how they think about life: fashion, food, and free-time.

Fashion

For young people anywhere in the world, looking good is a basic necessity, and in China, so-called "fast fashion" has become a baseline for hipness. In 2015, the market for fast fashion in China was worth nearly $80 billion. Uniqlo, which came to China in 2002, along with Zara and H&M, which entered a few years later are dominant players in the market. Sports gear brands are also very fashionable, with Nike and Adidas being very visible, with big stores on the most popular shopping streets, as well as smaller outlets near to their core target, for example in parks that attract many runners.

South-Korean and Japanese clothing fashion brands, such as Basic House or Muji, are also frequent favorites. Their quality and style are perceived as superior, and young Chinese are willing to pay a bit of a premium for their products.

For those with a slightly heavier wallet, fancy boutiques and high-end shops offer more personalized fashion. These stores aggregate by the dozens in the hipper areas of China's big cities, often just around the corner from main street flagship stores.

> In the words of Amy, one of the interviewees: *"I care more about quality, and less about brands."*

Fashion subcultures are readily apparent in this group, and three prominent ones offer a window into what is what is popular.

The first is "high-street style": it landed in China about five years ago from Britain. The overall idea is to offer a cool and elegant look without spending a fortune.

Besides the well-known fast fashion brands, a notable share of the high-street clothing market in China currently belongs to local retailers, such as Meters/Bonwe Group, which pushes a decidedly international style. The second is the Korean fashionista style, suitable for young women, dreamy but with enough street-smarts to thrive in the urban jungle. Girly and romantic, the trend has been fueled by actresses in Korean soap operas, which are much-loved by the female Chinese audience. The success of Korean dramas among Chinese women depends in great part on the attention to details—actresses are always impeccable in their make-up and dresses, the film sets always stylish and chic, and the dialogues mushy but intriguing.

A third might be termed "sports casual," which embraces habits like wearing running shoes about town. The boom in the sportswear industry in China has first to thank millennials, who are more and more embracing a healthy lifestyle. They are not only more informed and care about their diet, but genuinely like going to the gym and participating in sports—so much so that they want to show that off. Besides Nike and Adidas, the Chinese market is presently populated by a number of local brands, such as Li-Ning and Anta.

Food
When it comes to eating habits, the freshly graduated are diverse and sophisticated. And anyone with a WeChat account will note the constant stream of "foodie pictures" posted by this group—a habit so common that young people will often offer a joking apology while pulling out their camera during a meal. As one might infer from the pictures, this generation enjoys not just eating out but also trying new

food experiences. The prevalence of the habit has spawned its own lifestyle term, *chi huo* (吃货)—literally the union of "eat" and "merchandise."

Balancing off this rising love of the gourmet is the explosive growth of food delivery, fueled in part by the busy lives of not only this group but just about everyone living in Chinese cities. Eleme, Meituan and Sherpa are just a few of the many mobile apps used on a daily basis to have meals promptly delivered to home and office on a massive scale. But what sets this generation apart from others is the lack of the need to cook. With so many affordable options, they rarely spend time on home-cooked meals. And when they do, it is more out of pursuit of hobby than anything else—any good *chi huo* will now and then slip in a picture of a meal cooked herself, in addition to all the snapshots of restaurant meals.

Traditions also play a significant role in shaping their food preferences. When asked about their favorite food, almost all respondents named typical Chinese delicacies. For example, Andy indicated *kao rou* (烤肉), Chinese barbecue; Liu Fang the *mala xiang guo* (麻辣香锅) a spicy dish from Sichuan cuisine; and Wang Ping the popular *hong-shao rou* (红烧肉), a juicy pork-belly meat with a glistening red glaze. Although Western-style restaurants continue to proliferate in China, few Chinese people would list "hamburger" as their favorite meal.

Free-time

The availability and use of leisure time is of key importance to China's younger generation. Unlike older age groups, the freshly graduated are not often content to relax around the home, or sit idly in the park. With their keen-to-learn-new-things mindset, signing up for weekend classes to acquire a new skill is very popular. Given the increased focus on health compared to previous generations, and despite their busy lives, it is easy to spot them running early in the morning or attending late-evening spinning classes (gyms have exploded in popularity). Many universities have invested in sport facilities in the last few years as well, with many campuses offering their students large swimming pools, running circuits and basketball courts. Sport, movies and travel are the most frequent activities mentioned by young people, followed by eating out and listening to music.

In their own words:
Fen Fang: *"Travel, watching movies, and practicing yoga."*
Hua Ling: *"Swimming, playing ping-pong and badminton."*
Cheng Lei: *"Watching TV, sleeping, and playing games."*

Beyond Materialism

The coexistence of modern and traditional values is a principal characteristic of the young generation's value scheme. This is perhaps not so surprising, given that they were born into a world that was more "traditional," but have come of age in an economy and culture that is changing at light-speed. As such, wealth and success are perceived as essential to gaining social status, but are far from the only things that are valued. Respondents reported having strong guiding principles, frequently listing honesty, filial piety, integrity, gratitude and righteousness among their values. Some respondents also reported love for their country and the desire to contribute to national progress.

Conflicting values with the older generation
Interestingly, none of the interviewees for this chapter mentioned finding a soul mate as an important life-goal. This perhaps hints at an aspect of conflict they have with their parents' generation on attitudes toward love and marriage, one that has been leveraged by a variety of brands. For example, Coca-Cola's television commercial campaign for the 2017 Chinese New Year depicted a grandma asking her niece if she is going to get married, a common occurrence and source of stress for Chinese young adults around the holidays. Thanks to the vibe brought by the soft drink (mostly enjoyed by the granny), the question is left up in the air, and the young girl is saved the frustration of presumably having to answer in the negative.

Differing expectations around marriage are arguably the most visible generational conflict for the freshly graduated, but it is not the only one. Considering just how much China has changed in the last few decades, it is hardly surprising that young adults and their parents have different outlooks on life. In contrast to their parents and especially grandparents, this generation aspires to be freer, and to get more out of life.

In their own words:
Joy: *"I want to make my life fresher and more fun."*
Wang Fang: *"I don't want to dictate life to my future child too much, but give her encouragement, and respect her choices."*
Liu Wei: *"[I should] not get lost under the influence of all kinds of ideological trends, and carry out critical thinking."*

Differences in worldview also involve attitudes towards society in general. While the older generation cares more about political consciousness, the younger one is more focused on the economic interests of their country as well as environmental issues.

The young generation is looking for a new way of defining themselves, for a new idea of what it means to be modern. Life is, for the youngest adults, a constant process of discovery—for some, surely a roller coaster—rather than a flat and pre-written journey. New ideas can be critical of traditional Chinese life, such as too much family pressure, or the excessive weight of *guanxi* in determining the future. Their idea of modern, however, also encompasses criticism of Western culture, often perceived as being too superficial and dismissive. Chinese college graduates appreciate some key Western values like freedom, but at the same time, they see Western people as being too focused on enjoying their lives and minding their own business. If in the past, the Western lifestyle was idealized by many Chinese University students, experts have shown that this trend is changing.

> **In their own words:**
> Jie Xue: *"Fresh graduates in China have a different idea of modernity compared to the past. They sympathize with Western values, but do not idealize the Western world as before. They have nothing less. Their new identity is shaped towards innovation and technology, but also a sense of community and respect of traditional values."*

Expectations
Within the next five years, the young adults interviewed imagined themselves trapped in a successful and busy business

life, with meetings, a house mortgage and a tight schedule, with little free time—a telling outlook if there ever was one. In the near future, continuing education and professional certifications are recognized as key elements to survive job market competition. Only a few respondents mentioned "marriage and family" as a priority in the next five years.

In 10 years' time, or their mid-late thirties, their ideal life includes a healthy and happy family, a beautiful home, free time for traveling, an expensive car and trendy clothes. They see themselves professionally accomplished, laid-back and with a stable and prosperous life. This is the "Chinese dream" they are fighting for today.

In their own words:
Li Xiuying: *"I want to have a house that faces the sea, with spring flowers blossoming."*
Li Qiang: *"Financial freedom, though this may be a bit unrealistic. I hope that after ten years I will not be trapped by the economy, have my own family and have enough money to allow my parents to travel."*
Wang Yong: *"Be healthy, happy, and slow down the rate of aging."*
Li Min: *"Enjoy work, but not 15 hours a day; friends, a sincere partner, a Shiba dog."*

Challenges and fears
While some fresh graduates try to break out on their own, many are quite gloomy about their professional prospects. Despite their solid education and high expectations, the struggle to find a job is often perceived as exhausting. After China's economic growth began to slow around 2009, young graduates found themselves with the inausipcious

nickname of "*ant tribe*" (蚁族), as they tend to live together as if in nests on the outskirts of big cities.

Their fears may be overblown, however. Official data reports that the employment rate of the freshly graduated is more than 90%, compared with 82% for Europe and 96% in the United States in 2015. Additionally, many of the respondents were not only employed at the time of the interview, but generally satisfied with their current jobs. Other fears may be more realistic. Competition at the office, succeeding in the marriage market and skyrocketing housing prices were often cited. And although not captured by the interviews, Chinese graduates face an underemployment problem. According to MyCOS data, within a year of graduation, one out of four graduates has a salary below the average for migrant workers. This is particularly true for majors like history and literature.

The looming need to financially sustain the past generation while raising the next at the same time, is another important source of pressure. With the fast aging of the Chinese population, the increase in life expectancy, and the effects of the single-child policy, those born in the 1980s and 1990s feel the weight of a huge responsibility on their shoulders.

> **In their own words:**
> Bruce: *"Chase the material versus the spiritual."*

Interviewees were also asked about non-personal fears such as the national and global economic and political outlooks. While the recent slowdown of the Chinese economy causes some annoyance to the young generation, only a few expressed concern about China's domestic politics.

Conclusions and Takeaways

The number of China's freshly graduated steadily increases every year, and the group will keep on growing in the foreseeable future. Here are some takeaways in case you are thinking to target or hire them:

- With their pragmatic attitudes, their ability to learn fast and their open mindedness, hiring the freshly graduated will be an invaluable opportunity for companies to grow and to better understand the Chinese market. However, without a clear career development plan, their commitment may not last long.

- Always looking for new stimuli and improved skills, companies should offer them the possibility of acquiring new competencies.

- New business opportunities should focus on facilitating their busy lives: health and time-saving apps, and stress management apps, for example, are in demand.

- It is also recommended to use promotion strategies if this is your target, especially with group buying.

Fresh Graduates – Two Stories

Maria and Emily 29 and 27, founders of GoEast, a Chinese language school

Maria and I started GoEast, a professional Chinese language school, in the spring of 2012. At the time, Maria had just earned her Master's degree, receiving several offers from big corporations. I was still in my second year of graduate school. Both of our backgrounds are in linguistics, which is quite far from business.

I first saw a link between my professional field and business after I received a piece of advice from a respected economist at Fudan University: "Entrepreneurs are born, not taught. You can do it." Motivated and determined, we entered and subsequently won the Shanghai Innovation and Entrepreneurship Competition, receiving our first funding from the Shanghai government. Despite the win we only recruited 33 students during our first year and suffered great financial loss. Doubts arose from everywhere: friends, family and even ourselves. Almost every time I spoke with my mother she asked me, "When are you going to get a real job?" Under the greatest pressure and anxiety we ever experienced, we told ourselves to hold on one more year and to work hard and enjoy this as much as we could.

In 2017, we now have a core team of 12 management people and 94 teachers. Looking back, starting up GoEast was probably the best decision we ever made. As young entrepreneurs we lacked resources, insight and experience, but we had lower opportunity costs, greater flexibility and adaptability. We had to learn fast to grow rapidly.

We are now in an era with more transparency and opportunities thanks to the internet. For our company, this means we need to take advantage of how people connect online to better help our students learn Chinese language and culture. This is our challenge and opportunity to become a modern tech education company.

Morgan, 28, graduate of Shanghai International Studies University (SISU)

After graduation, I got a job in the university working as a foreign affairs officer. For many traditional Chinese, it is a "sweet job" as it is stable and offers a good social reputation. I was also glad of it at that time. In the first year, I also felt very challenged because we were short-handed.

But it became different as the second year started. The work became repetitive, and I felt I was not growing. Therefore, it occurred to me to find another job. However, quitting a stable job is not easy, especially for a woman over 27. There is a huge dilemma to face in your career when you are old but still junior. You may encounter a great number of colleagues who are younger, energetic and cheap to hire. Meanwhile, you would also face tremendous peer pressure as your classmates are already junior managers.

Considering all of these things, I spent a very long time making the decision whether to leave or stay. One of my friends gave me the final push by saying that the longer you stay in your comfort zone, the less capacity you have for change. You will suffer more of the same pain year by year. And then all of a sudden, I got enough courage to face the possible future frustrations, and I quit.

My new job now is working as a news producer. It is contract work, and the benefits are much worse than the old job. But I never felt happier. Every day has something new. I find news and produce stories. Every day is a new experience, and I learn from it. And all the concerns I worried over turned out to be not that daunting. There is much bigger world outside than you can imagine.

CHAPTER SEVEN

The Comfortably Elderly

Francis Bassolino and Forrest Cranmer

IN AUGUST 1957, in Anhui Province, not far from China's east coast, Zhang Ling gave birth to a girl she named Xiao, or "Filial." Three years later she gave birth to another girl she called Yu, "Lucky."* Both girls led an early life that they still refer to as *ku*, or bitter. Hunger and struggle were all that life seemed to offer these girls in their first decade or so. Anhui was near the center of Mao's Great Leap Forward campaign, 1958-62, which resulted in millions of deaths, mostly from starvation primarily caused by administrative ineptitude.

In adolescence, food was more abundant, but this period brought ten years of political and social chaos with the Cultural Revolution, which began in 1966. Following the death of Mao in 1976, and the ascendance of Deng Xiaoping, who began "reform and opening up" in 1978, Chinese society began to change, slowly at first, steadily delivering economic opportunities and better lives.

But the early trauma left an indelible mark: throughout their lives, Filial and Lucky kept to their father's principle of saving as much as possible, because one could never tell when China might devolve yet again into chaos.

Filial, the older daughter, missed the opportunity to attend college as she came of age during the Cultural Revolution when universities were closed. At 18, she married a

115

man from a nearby village and took to a traditional role, working on the farm and taking care of the children, being an obedient and dutiful wife, daughter and daughter-in-law. She saved what little money that she could, but early on her world was mostly a cashless society in which people by and large lived off the land, bartering with neighbors.

Lucky followed a different path. An excellent student, she gained entrance to Fudan University, a leading university in Shanghai, and later landed a job at the Bank of China in Shanghai. She married her classmate, an English major who liked to call himself Peter ("the Great," she often jokes). Peter also took up work in Shanghai, at a trading company that was focused on textile exports to the United States and Europe.

For Lucky and Peter, life seemed to be nothing but an onward and upward march, with each year bringing more prosperity and opportunity. Peter began to travel internationally for work and he was exposed to many new ideas and opportunities. In the 1990s, he and a colleague opened their own trading company, bought for a pittance from a bankrupt state-owned enterprise, and took over several textile factories that fed the seemingly insatiable demand from the US big-box retail market.

The success enabled Lucky to go back to school at 33, but this time to study for an MBA at the University of Chicago. She thereafter joined Morgan Stanley's investment banking division. By 2005, just as China's real estate boom was gaining momentum, Lucky and Peter had acquired multiple apartments in Shanghai, attaining a net worth they are too bashful to reveal.

Many of their classmates and co-workers also benefited from fortuitous timing and location. Now 60, the conversation with Lucky's classmate's involve such things as: buying property in the United States; the luxury retirement villages popping up across China; vacationing in Turkey (because Paris now has too many Chinese!).

For Zhang the Filial, life turned out much differently. Years of hard labor, working in the fields in Anhui, and then working in Shenzhen for some time in a factory, left her with chronic illness and sore joints. Her husband recently passed on, due to cancer from his chain smoking and difficult jobs both in the fields and in a metal stamping company in Ningbo where no one was concerned about employee safety. Recently, she went to live with her son in Hefei, but it never felt like home there. She couldn't get along with her daughter-in-law and always felt like she was in the way, no matter that she did all the cooking and cleaning as well as the child-rearing for her grandchild who is now in high school.

Eventually she moved back to her hometown so that she could be near friends and relatives and away from the relentless construction and noise of Hefei. She worries that in a few years, she will have to go and live with her son or go into the wretched old-age home offered by the government. Her meager savings was mostly spent on the last six months of care for her husband.

Lucky tries to pay for most everything, but Filial just can't seem to accept her sister's generosity. They are just so different: they have nothing in common and she is too bitter and proud.

* *Filial and Lucky are fictional characters based on conversations with survey respondents from numerous projects in areas covering the life of seniors in China including financial services, entertainment, healthcare, senior living and tourism, to name a few sources of insight gained over the past thirty years.*

Gilded Age of Golden Years

What we termed the "comfortably elderly" is an emerging market segment that is vastly different from earlier retiree groups, in terms of attitudes toward consumption and in raw spending power. Recent and upcoming retirees are orders of magnitude wealthier than earlier generations, having been able to reap the rewards of China's economic boom. As China rapidly ages, this market segment will continue to grow in size for the next 15 years, and with it come exciting opportunities in products and services geared toward the needs of the aged and affluent.

It is important to bear in mind the vast size of China and the relative differences in standard of living, not to mention life outcomes—as seen with Lucky and Filial. This book being what it is, the focus here is on the Luckys of China. The survey data in this chapter is based on survey responses from around 80 members of her cohort.

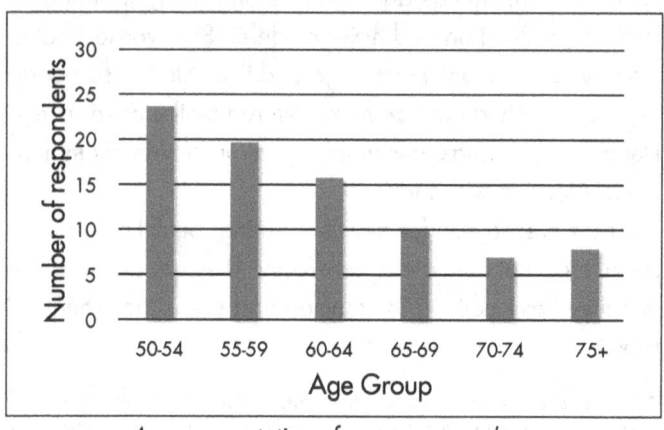

Age segmentation of survey respondents

As seen with riveting clarity in the lives of the Zhang sisters, there is a clear generational difference between those born prior to 1960 and those post-1960. Chinese born prior to 1960 came of age during a tumultuous time in China, and these individuals viscerally understand the unspeakable events that China witnessed in the mid-20th century. Starvation, war, political campaigns, betrayal of family members and an overall breakdown of order were familiar scenes throughout their childhood and young-adult years. These formative early life experiences have left strong marks upon their attitudes toward life. Individuals of this era tend to be frugal, practical and conservative when it comes to consumption of any kind, except in education, healthcare and real estate (if they can afford it), where they can be overly aggressive, as these items are perceived as investments that will secure a better future.

Apart from these necessities and investments, money was for saving, never for spending. These individuals may have saved in excess of 35% of their income over their entire lives, sometimes even above 50%. They therefore have a comfortable nest egg, but are disinclined not to spend on much beyond the necessary.

For those born after 1960, such suffering may be a vague childhood memory, comfortably erased by a national school curriculum that tries to expunge this horrible period from the historical record. For most people aged 55 years old or younger, each year has brought increasing wealth and comfort. The "New Elderly" came of age as opportunities exploded, during multiple decades of massive sustained growth, when real estate prices have increased by as much as 10-fold in some regions, when salaries increased in line with, or even exceeded GDP growth—when millionaires were made.

Chinese of this generation have the affluence to afford their child's educational needs, as well as the ability and inclination to treat themselves to the rest, so long as they leave behind a nest egg for the next generation. This is a marked shift in attitude. While many still have relatively conservative spending habits, they are far more relaxed than their predecessors. Many take up hobbies such as learning to play a musical instrument, dancing, painting, hiking and traveling. As they tend to retire earlier—generally 55 for women and 60 for men—they have the energy these days to enjoy themselves.

Among both affluent and not, the rhythms of retired life tend to be similarly simple. Many retirees start each morning in the nearest park and spend a significant amount of time there practicing Taichi, dancing, chatting or exercising. They have simple tastes and limited expenses. Many still do their own cooking as its far cheaper than eating out and many do not trust the cleanliness of restaurants.

Soon-to-be-retirees are expected to have a similar daily arc of spending their mornings in the park or elsewhere in their neighborhood. These retirees have known years of growing prosperity, bringing with it a greater willingness to spend on themselves and desire to explore the globe. While older generations are happy to spend each day as they did the last, new generations of retirees are increasingly inclined to see the world and enjoy the amenities of their choosing.

Aging and Urbanizing

Geographically, there is a major shift of the elderly population underway. Population figures in 2015 show that were 200 million elderly people split evenly between urban and rural. But because of the more general rural-to-urban shift, by 2030, the urban elderly population will more than double to 230 million while rural locations will only grow by 30% to 130 million.

This is highly significant because urbanites have much different attitudes toward consumption and much deeper pockets. So not only is there a significant capacity to spend, there is also a greater willingness to do so.

Urban living also brings with it changes to long-held traditions. Congregating under one roof, especially after a grandchild is born, is something of a timeless ideal, reflected in numerous proverbs about family and prosperity. While these traditions die hard, and many parents, especially those in the countryside, still wish to live with their children, this is increasingly unfeasible in major urban centers. Even for those wealthy enough to afford a 300-square meter apartment, (enough for four bedrooms, and 2-3-bathrooms), it may not be desirable to live with one's parents. Urbanites have grown accustomed to living in their own homes. (Grandparents may, however, stay temporarily immediately after a grandchild is born in order to lend a hand.)

In Shanghai, the majority of retirees also prefer to live on their own. The inclination is to live in close proximity to their children, while still being able to enjoy their own space. When prodded on the topic, a typical response was: "Because I then retain a sense of independence." Some are more blunt: "Four adults and one child living in a 170 sq. meter apartment—I think not."

Fears: Past and Present
A common, but mostly unspoken, concern for older Chinese

is stability and security—a relic of their own difficult experiences, as well as the cultural memory of the previous generations who experienced decades of near-unbroken hardship starting in the mid-1800s: the downfall of the Manchu Dynasty, two world wars, a civil war and the self-inflicted damage of the 1950s and 1960s.

The need for financial security (as well as a lack of financial service products such as loans) is a big part of what drove the almost compulsive saving habits of elderly Chinese, along with preparing for dowries or the like. Soon-to-be retirees are motivated to save more out of the desire to live comfortably in their old age. However, a certain pragmatism still unites them. Asked what they would do if they suddenly got RMB 10 million ($1.5 million), the overwhelming majority would buy a new house or invest. Ask a 30-40 year old Chinese the same question and the answer may include things such as global travel and luxury expenditures.

While many working-age Chinese may not pay too close attention to their health, it becomes an obsession for many towards old age. This focus ties into concerns about the state of health care services, food security, and medical treatment quality, reliability and availability. It is common for many Chinese to visit practitioners of traditional Chinese medicine before opting to pay a visit to a crowded public hospital.

Many urban elderly also dread being a burden on their own children. Even if their child wanted to take care of them when they themselves are no longer capable of doing so, their child would be unlikely to have the time or energy. Once again, modern economic realities make it unfeasible for children to adhere to traditional precepts of filial piety. This terror of being a burden is tied into the fear of being removed from their child. In the same vein, not seeing their grandchildren is also cause for concern.

Other personal fears include loneliness, boredom, and being scammed. A common complaint amongst elderly Chinese across China is feeling lonely. This is especially true for those Chinese grandparents who live with their children far removed from their hometown, because it uproots them from their social network of friends and extended family. Many elderly Chinese find this situation intolerable in the long run because they have no one to talk with, their child is busy working and the grandchild is in school for most of the day and no longer requires chaperoning. For such reasons, some elderly Chinese will choose to live in their hometowns or opt for an elderly care institution as a way to remedy the feeling of intolerable loneliness. This social idleness also drives uptake of hobbies.

Surveys of retirees and soon-to-be-retired individuals show higher levels of discretionary spending among those under 65. While they remain conservative, even a small shift toward greater discretionary spending is significant. What is more significant is that our research finds increasingly younger generations are more willing to spend on themselves on everything from manicures to Starbucks coffee. As the urban elderly population continues to grow, there will be ever more rapid increases in discretionary spending.

Hidden Purchasing Power
Simply put, elderly Chinese purchasing power has increased drastically. In 2015, more than 50% of seniors had an annual household income of more than RMB 162,000 ($25,000). As previously mentioned, many are avid sav-

ers, with average savings rates still above 50%, many have been able to continue to invest.

While it is uncommon for senior Chinese above the age of 65 to invest their money outside of fixed income securities offered by top-tier banks, it is now common amongst younger cohorts. Those belonging to the 65-and-older group will have saved all their earnings in one or two bank accounts. Many are too suspicious of financial products, or simply unfamiliar with them, to consider aggressive investment products, and even local public equities are mostly viewed as gambling. The logic is that putting the money in a bank account is safe, while investment outside of real estate carries undue risk.

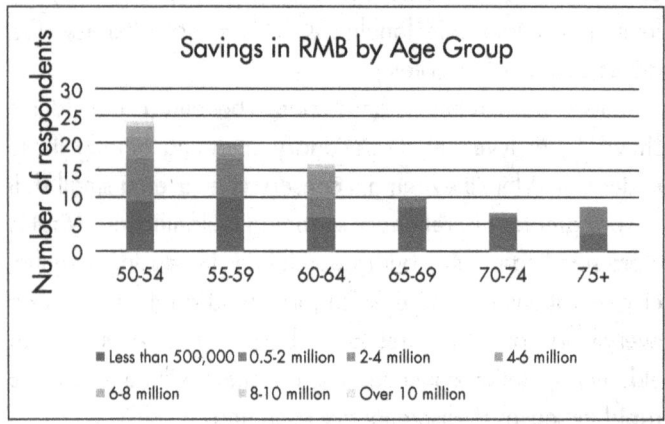

Note: Chinese are very sensitive about their savings. Friends do not ask friends about how much they have saved. These figures are both estimations and claims made by respondents that give a rough idea of the savings of older Chinese. Seniors may have over RMB 1 million tucked away in a bank account, but they will tell you they don't even have RMB 500,000. Children are often clueless to how much their parents have saved, as are friends.

As a result, younger generations have been capturing greater returns on their earnings. Many interviewees reportedly had less than RMB 500,000 ($75,000) in savings, but it is not unreasonable to suppose that many of these individuals were understating their savings. At just a 30% savings rate for workers averaging RMB 5,000 ($750) per month over their careers nets RMB 720,000 ($108,000) over 40 years of work. Keep in mind that many might have been able to save much more (and there is significant gray income that is not reported), which makes a total savings of over RMB 1 million ($150,000) readily attainable.

The other important source of wealth is housing. During the late 1980s, China phased out its *fenpei* policy of helping workers to buy out their own homes. This policy had enabled many workers of the elder age cohort to much more easily afford a home, which, as discussed earlier, will have since seen significant appreciation in value, particularly in major urban centers. High savings and owning their home outright puts many seniors in a secure financial position. Furthermore, these seniors are entirely capable of living off their pensions, which in Beijing and Shanghai average over RMB 3,000 ($450) per month. They may even receive a stipend from their children, and wealthier seniors garner additional money from renting out a second apartment.

Urban 50-60 year olds are generally even more financially secure than the current seniors. It is common for the younger cohort to own 2-4 homes outright or with less than 20% leverage. With salaries that were higher than the average, plus investment income, many have savings rates well over 30% of their income. Additionally, these individuals will have diversified their investments to include bonds, financial products, funds and stocks. This means many will have seen greater returns on investment than simply sticking money into one bank account at the 3-5% interest rate available from standard products over the past few decades.

For retired seniors, the only times they are incapable of living entirely off their pensions is if medical treatment costs spike in the case of an emergency. A few elderly report that the pension just covers food and medical expenses—these elderly seniors will only draw on their savings in times of absolute necessity. This is a stark contrast from the upcoming retirees who are inclined to enjoy their years of retirement with travel and leisure. Upcoming seniors are by no means intent on spending the entirety of their earnings and savings, but they will certainly have higher levels of discretionary spending.

Senior urbanites' expenditures can be summarized as: paying for medical care as prescribed, vacations on an annual to biannual basis, paying for their child's accommodation upon marriage (if they haven't already done so), education expenditures for their grandchildren, and entertainment when desired. We expect discretionary spending among soon-to-be retirees to be greater than earlier generations, but these upcoming seniors will tend towards pragmatism when making purchases and occasional pleasure spends. Older generations may only spend in items that are deemed absolutely necessary, whereas newer generations will spend on useful items and enjoyable products and/or services. Ever younger generations show an increasingly relaxed attitude toward consumption. And 35-50 year olds surely have a clear accounting of the significant inheritance that is coming their way.

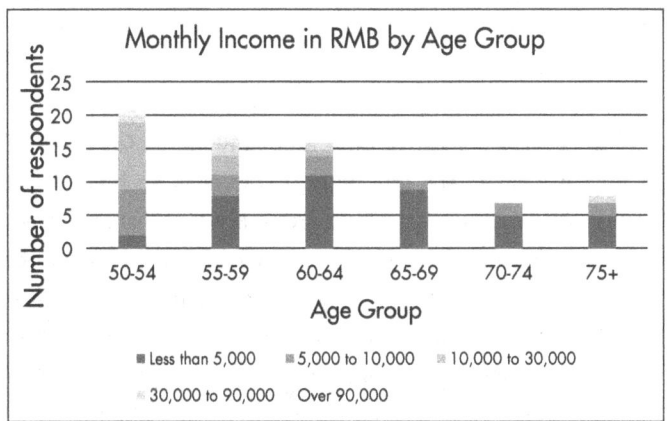

Note: Virtually every retiree surveyed draws primarily from their pension of RMB 2000-3000 depending on location and doesn't reflect their income prior to retiring.

Old Folks, New Opportunities

The comfortably elderly are growing in wealth and number. China's rapid economic growth over the last three decades has made many Chinese, particularly urbanites, very affluent. Ever-increasing material comforts have eased some of their rigid conservative behaviors. Gone are the days when one's savings were a sacred treasure only to be utilized in emergencies.

Upcoming retirees today save with the explicit purpose of being able to enjoy their retirement. While visiting the park daily will still be a common feature for many elderly, new retirees will be periodically seeing what excitement the world at large has to offer. Those born prior to 1960 generally spend only on themselves when it is absolutely necessary, i.e. healthcare. Those born after 1960, will spend on amenities that bring them joy, whether that be new clothes, spa visits, music classes, travel abroad, etc. This affluent set of upcoming retirees represents a huge market opportunity. These individuals have both the time and money to spend on goods and services that pique their interests.

Traveling is a high priority for many urban Chinese set to retiree. But where and how to travel is so much of a mystery that the majority favor group travel. Most only have a vague idea about where to go, what to see, how to get there and where to eat. Many fear traveling alone or just with their spouse. When asking interviewees about different travel services that interested them, many liked the idea of small-group travel packages that offer greater freedom, more authentic experiences, and greater intimacy. Many Chinese feel that language and cultural barriers dictate that you need a guide. There are considerable opportunities and niche markets to capture amongst elderly Chinese.

Healthcare, and especially preventative healthcare, also offer unique opportunities. Many Chinese do not have a clear understanding about what constitutes healthy habits and what is going to be best for their bodies and minds, both in terms of physical and mental activities. Fitness classes geared toward seniors at a reasonable price would interest seniors looking to maintain a healthy body. Most are uninterested in paying for a private trainer who may charge RMB 150 ($22) or more per lesson. Medicines, tonics, nutrition in any and all forms will continue to have a market in China.

Elderly care is the most obvious opportunity that is attracting capital from large investment firms in China and globally. Middle-class elderly are not interested in the state-sponsored elderly care facilities where 6-8 people sleep in the same room. Such institutions are largely for those who are infirm and cannot afford private care. Many interviewees noted that once they are incapable of looking after themselves, they would opt first to live at home with 24-hour care and, second to move to an elderly care institution so as not to be burden upon their children. Many of these urban elderly have the means to afford full-service care that includes in-house medical services. And many of these seniors will receive funds from children. While filial piety may look as if it is vanishing in the cities, Chinese people still wish the best for their parents and want them to receive excellent care and treatment.

Seniors are also interested in activities that they can socialize over, even meet new friends. In elderly care facilities, having a recreation center and frequent social events is an absolute must for middle-class seniors. While these seniors may not know what service or product allows them to meet and socialize, this is an opportunity to become part of the fabric of their lives. Fortunately, upcoming seniors are increasingly comfortable with using cellphones and tablets, which opens the possibility of creating an innovative digital solution for connecting seniors.

Overall, it is clear that the comfortably elderly is an emerging market with affluence, time and increasing purchasing power, coupled with increasingly open attitudes towards consumption for themselves. This is an exciting time to begin tapping into the "new old market."

CHAPTER EIGHT

China's Generation Z: Growing Up After 2010

Elisabeth de Gramont

IT IS SUMMER in Shanghai, and Xiao Nuo is starting at a new school in September. She is excited to ride the school bus for the first time, but nervous about having to sit still in class listening to the teacher. She just turned six years old, but Xiao Nuo is already a veteran of busy schedules—she has had three years of formal schooling, 8:30am to 4pm, plus extra English classes on Tuesdays and Thursdays since she was four. And her mother does everything she can beyond that to expose her to different people, environments and ideas. She has been to Hong Kong, Japan and to Shanghai Disneyland. She feels as comfortable dragging her Elsa suitcase (from the hit animated movie *Frozen*) through an airport as she does singing the movie's theme song "Let it Go," in English.

Xiao Nuo represents the next generation of urban Chinese kids—privileged and sophisticated, and fully exposed to the world even before they get to primary school. She and her peers are also at the crux of the tensions between the progressive parenting attitudes of China's new upper-middle class, and a traditional education system that still prizes rote memorization and quantifiable scores. This conflict has been simmering since the "post-1990s" generation started coming of age in the mid-2000s. But with parents who they themselves were the first generation of privileged, single children, the "post-2010s" generation embodies the ambitions and values of China's future.

A Happy Childhood, with All the Tools for Success

> *"I want my son to thrive in this competitive world."*
> *"I want him to understand the real world."*
> *"I want him to grow up seeing me as a friend,*
> *not a parent."*

These are the desires of today's young post-1980s parents. As the first generation of single children, they grew up with the weight of opportunity on their shoulders. They could be more educated, more successful, and have more colorful lives than their own parents. But with no template for how to achieve this success, their own childhoods were primarily defined by long school days and one goal—to pass the college entrance exam, or *gaokao*, a notoriously difficult two-day affair.

Fast-forward to 2017. Now that they have their own kids, this generation has a new definition for what "success" can be in today's China, one that is not purely academic and which heavily influences what type of parents they want to be.

"When I was a kid, my dad never admitted if he didn't understand something. On the contrary, I feel very interested when my kid teaches me something I do not know. Sometimes he is my source of inspiration"—*Lin, father of an eight-year-old in Shanghai*

In the past fifteen years, the biggest evolution in parenting attitudes has come from parents born in the late-1970s and 1980s wanting to reverse the "top-down," authoritarian approach that their own parents took. While the traditional idea of "tiger mom, wolf dad," *a la* Amy Chua, is still engrained as a stereotype of Chinese parents, today's younger moms and dads are aspiring to a "new way" of interacting with their kids. "I want to be friends with my daughter, not just a parent," is now the prevailing mindset of parents of the preschool set.

> "My daughter and I are like sisters—we get dressed up together and gossip together"—*Chen Yi, mother of a six-year-old in Shanghai*

While these young, urban, Chinese parents are without a doubt inspired by a positive perception of "Western" education as fostering more egalitarian relationships between children and adults, they are perhaps more directly looking for a change from the way they were raised. They grew up with a strong sense of family and community, but with academic performance as the key benchmark for their success. Now as parents themselves, they want a more balanced relationship with their kids, with more dialogue and fewer restrictions.

But these new parenting attitudes are not so much about rebelling against the older generation as about seizing the new opportunities and sophisticated lifestyles available to them. Although it is still the norm for grandparents to be charged with daily childcare while mom and dad are at work, their influence is limited to matters of nutrition and hygiene. When it comes to play and education, it is the parents who dictate the program. Based on their own upbringing, and a lower education level of the older generation, there is little faith that grandparents are able to prepare their kids for the modern world.

> "I won't leave my parents in charge of my son's education, because they just spoil him and don't know how to teach him"—*Wei, mom of 18-month old in Chengdu*

Online meme of kids raised by grandparents vs parents
The caption reads: Raised by Mom & Dad (爸妈带) vs. Raised by grandparents (奶奶带)

The parents of today's toddlers grew up as China was opening up, and without the references that drive nostalgic consumption among millennial parents in the West. Mickey Mouse, always a pioneer, only arrived on state-run CCTV in 1986. Star Wars, which has re-energized its brand in the West by catering to thirty-somethings reliving their childhood fantasies, has faltered in China without an anchor in 1980s pop culture.

China's post-1980s parents are therefore on a journey of discovery together with their kids, looking to indulge in new entertainment and experiences. They want to enjoy the new options available and seek out "fun" experiences that they wish they had had as kids. Many of these young parents were raised with their grandparents as primary caretakers, also fueling the desire for a different relationship and more bonding experiences with their own children.

"I didn't have such cool toys when I was a kid. But I wish I had, so I buy a lot for my son." —*Wang Yi, dad of nine-year-old in Beijing*

"Parent and child" activities from book readings, arts and crafts classes, and sporting events are booming. As a center for family weekend entertainment, shopping malls across China are capitalizing on this need, hosting ever more exciting exhibits and events inspired by Chinese and Western entertainment franchises, ranging from Sesame Street to "Walking with Dinosaurs," which features animatronic dinosaurs fit for a museum. Theme parks are similarly exploding. Shanghai Disneyland opened in 2016 at a cost $5.5 billion, and the Chinese market for theme parks is expected to become the world's largest by 2020.

Beyond shopping malls and theme parks, the desire to share fun experiences with kids is also being reflected in China's tourism boom. Goldman Sachs estimates that two-thirds of the 120 million outbound tourists from China in 2015 were 18-35 year olds, a key demographic that is now having children and traveling with them.

> "I took my baby to Sanya (on Hainan Island in southern China)—it is an opportunity to open her eyes to new places, and for her to realize the world outside is not all the same"—*Zhou, mom of two-year-old in Chengdu*

But even as fun, play, and being friends with their children are top priorities for parents, the methods they turn to are undeniably tied to helping them to thrive and succeed in a competitive world. Travel, in fact, helps to serve this purpose. For kids of all ages, parents are seeing travel as a way to open their eyes to the world and cultivate the adaptability and exposure that will be essential for their future success.

There is a strong sense that today's society is more complex, and there are more skills required to thrive. In the 1990s, getting a college degree could more or less guarantee a stable income, high social status, and a comfortable life. Kids in school were not just pushed by their parents, but also by a clear message from society as a whole—get a good score on the *gaokao*, get into college, and you'll be fine.

Today's school-aged kids are faced with a more complex reality because the definition of "success," not to mention the path that leads to it, is no longer so clear. While there is more pressure to acquire diverse skills, there are also more "Plan B" options for those who don't succeed in traditional channels. Parents are constantly forming and then re-evaluating their parenting philosophy, especially when it comes to managing their child's activities and academics.

One thing is clear, however: Chinese parents today are now experiencing a fundamental tension between conflicting desires. They don't want to give their child external pressure, but they also want them to cultivate an internal drive to succeed.

Play Hard, Learn Hard

"Yi is the busiest person in our family! Every Tuesday and Thursday, she has painting and swimming after school. On Saturday she has English in the morning and Lego class in the afternoon"—*Wang, mom of a six-year-old in Shanghai*

Although Chinese parents value "play" and "fun" more than ever before, there is a strong sense that playtime should also be an opportunity for self-improvement and cultivating skills. Even before age two, toddlers in China's big cities, especially first-tier cities like Beijing and Shanghai, are being enrolled in a variety of classes to develop social, intellectual, physical, and artistic skills. This is a key driver of China's booming early education market, which is projected to reach $52 billion in 2020.

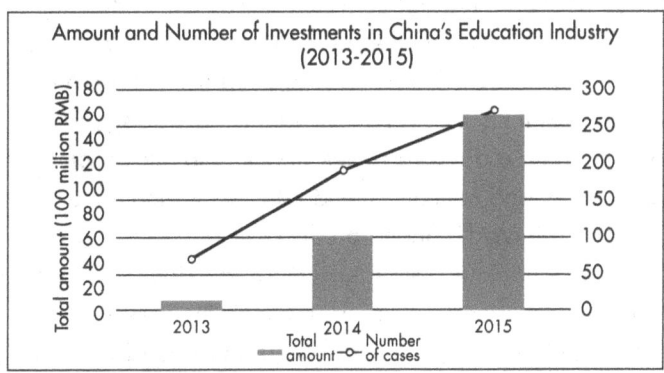

Demand for things like early-childhood education in China has helped drive massive investment in the education sector
Source: Deloitt

Even before primary school, a child might be enrolled in as many as four different weekly classes. Popular ones include painting, piano, English, and Lego building. From a parent's perspective, these classes are just another type of play, both more fun and productive than sitting alone at home with their toys.

But there is also an inevitable aspect of competition. Although most parents say they only want to give their child exposure to different interests, there is often a nagging concern that they aren't doing enough. Xing Min, a mom in Shanghai whose daughter has a lighter weekend schedule than her kindergarten classmates, says, "I feel like if my daughter has 1.5 days free on the weekend, I'm letting her fall behind."

Because these kids are enrolled in extra-curricular classes at such a young age, and their parents value classroom time as play time, free play with toys is drastically reduced by the time they start primary school. It is little wonder that Mattel announced a joint-venture with Fosun Group, a Chinese conglomerate and owner of Club Med, to launch "play and learn" clubs across China starting in 2018 to capitalize on the need for more organized play. The first new Mattel-Fosun "play and learn" club is planned for Shanghai's Bund waterfront with a 15,000-square-foot area housing a daycare center, playground, classrooms for early childhood education, and retail space featuring Mattel and Club Med-branded products.

Another unique "side effect" of the focus on more achievement-oriented, organized play is the impact on how kids socialize. Parents know that getting ahead in society and business requires more than just a high IQ. Stories abound in the news and in social media of kids who were at the top of their class but can't hold down a regular job for lack of social skills. So the stakes for "socialization" are high as well. Parents want their kids to start learning how to make friends and feel confident in social situations as young as possible.

> "A good personality is important to make a person thrive in society" —Ying, mom of an eight-month-old in Chengdu

This emphasis on building social skills and EQ (emotional intelligence) usually starts with organic encouragement—taking a baby to the park to see and meet other children, encouraging a toddler to say hello to people on the street. From age three or four, EQ "education" becomes more systematic, with classes like "public speaking" becoming popular with preschool students.

One of the results of this is that kids today are becoming great networkers—they know how to make friends easily, and have multiple social circles, including their neighbors, classmates, family friends, and friends from extra classes. But they have fewer deep relationships with one or two "best friends."

Although kindergarten is increasingly filled with extra classes and busy schedules for small children, the goal for parents is to give their child exposure to as many different things as possible so that they can cultivate their own interests. Even though social pressure exists, it is more about providing opportunities to their child and less about making them conform to specific benchmarks for achievement.

Primary school, on the other hand is a turning point for

kids and parents. Schedules become even more intense as extra-curricular classes shift from "fun" (Lego, painting) to academic (Olympic math, extra Chinese).

A typical schedule for a first-grader in Shanghai looks something like this:

Weekdays
Before School: half hour of English revision + half hour of piano
8am-3:30pm: School
4pm-5:30pm: Extra classes: dance 2x/week and English 2x/week
5:30-6:30: Dinner
6:30-8pm: Homework and piano practice

Saturdays
8:30-2:30pm: Chinese, logical thinking, and public speaking class

Parents have a perpetual struggle. Not only is this schedule grueling for their child, but it creates an increasing amount of work for themselves, as they spend their own time checking homework and organizing schedules. Far from feeling like "tiger parents," most parents say they don't expect too much from their children, and just hope they can stay "above average."

The only problem is that "average" feels impossible to achieve without extra classes. If everyone else is doing it, it becomes a basic requirement.

"As long as my son is above average, I'm happy—but the bar for 'average' is getting higher every day"
—*Huang Hong, mom of a nine-year-old in Shanghai*

Easing the Burden

Schools and the government are well aware of the pressure that children are under, and in 2013 the Ministry of Education instituted a number of reforms at the primary level aiming to "ease the burden" (减负) for students and parents.

However, it has become a common refrain among parents that the policies are actually aimed at "easing the burden" of the schools and teachers, while shifting the burden to parents. One measure that sounds good on paper but has created grumbling among parents is the policy of "strictly forbidding extra classes." Basically, public schools and their teachers are no longer supposed to offer extra tutoring or instruction after school hours.

Instead of eliminating a culture of after-school academic work, the result has been that parents feel more pressure to seek outside private classes at extra cost without the convenience of keeping their kids on school grounds. Similarly, China has weighed rules banning homework for young children. But "appropriate experiential activities" like handicrafts or going on special field trips usually require more parental involvement.

The struggle to truly reform the school system and ease the pressure of schoolwork on young children is emblematic of larger cultural tensions in China. These post-1980s parents want to prioritize providing opportunity and exposure over quantifiable academic success, but still see education as the key to getting ahead.

Huang Hong in Shanghai says, "I don't push him to be at the top of his class, but at the end of the day, doing well in school is still the easiest way to get ahead if you don't already have family money or connections."

Searching for the middle ground is not easy—even if kids are being told that "good enough" is okay, it isn't clear to most parents and kids what "enough" really means.

Compete Against Yourself

"I always tell my daughter that she shouldn't compare herself to others in her class, that it doesn't matter who is better"—*Chen Yi, mom of a six-year-old in Shanghai*

One marked change from school life in the 1980s and 1990s is that schools no longer publicly rank children's grades for each classroom. This is in line with the belief of many of today's parents' that their kids should not be driven by competition with others.

However, there is also a clear hope among parents that their children will find the internal drive to push themselves. While schools no longer publish student rankings, teachers are still explicit about publicly praising students who are at the top of their class. The impact is clear when kids come home to tell their parents who did well that day. If a preschooler comes home to report that her classmate "Xing Xing already knows how to write her own name," most parents would be gratified that it makes their own child feel pressure to do better.

Ultimately, today's Chinese parents are hoping that their child doesn't feel too much pressure, but also believe it is critical for them to develop their own self-drive to survive in the modern world and workforce. When asked what values they hope their child can cultivate, persistence (坚持) and a willingness to continue progressing (进步) are top of the list. In order to get there, parents are doing what they can to expose their children to as many opportunities as possible—from math to art—because in today's world, there are many paths to success.

A Preview of the Future

Although it is impossible to know how these post-2010s kids will turn out as adults, we already see signs in the new attitudes of today's teenagers—China's "Generation Z"—or those born after 1995. These teens grew up with more educated and open-minded parents than the post-1980s crowd, and now have almost unlimited access to digital media and information (firewalls notwithstanding). Even though their high school schedules are very similar to those born in the 1980s and early 1990s (i.e. millennials), the amount of pressure they feel to excel academically is markedly different.

Most are still working toward the *gaokao*, but they no longer see that as the capstone of their teenage years. In fact, there is an increasing sense that they have many options outside the academic path. Even down to third and forth-tier cities, teenagers born in the late 1990s feel they have plenty of options for the future. While the entrepreneurial success of Jack Ma and Alibaba was aspirational but distant for the generation of the 1980s, most of today's urban teens have at least one friend or acquaintance making a living through their online persona or commercial savvy.

As non-traditional career paths emerge, universities are offering new types of majors that can appeal to the less academic-minded. Yiwu Industrial & Commercial College in Zhejiang, not far from Shanghai, offers a major in "Modeling & Etiquette," which is pitched to students as a full course on how to go viral online. In addition to dance, photography and make-up, other classes include "network marketing" and "public relations etiquette"—a complete toolkit to becoming a "KOL," that is "Key Opinion Leader," those digital media personalities who have made careers out of being online taste makers and brand ambassadors.

Kids in China have been under pressure to excel for a long time. Although the manifestations may be changing from long school hours with strict teachers to weekends filled with parent-driven extra-curricular activities, the way they are being raised also presents great opportunity. And though the education system may not reform quickly, the tone and style of education in schools is clearly changing. As these young kids who grew up attending public speaking classes become more opinionated and impatient, teachers are also being forced to adapt their teaching style to be more engaging, and even entertaining.

Middle school students like Li Zhizhi from Sichuan province in China's southwest, are becoming increasingly demanding of their teachers, telling us, "Our math teacher is everyone's favorite, he will use '*Duanzi*' (short idioms used to tell a joke) to stimulate the class atmosphere, and he constantly changes his tone and volume of voice based on the content to hold our attention for longer."

With a combination of skills cultivated by their parents from a young age—being comfortable in various environments, being exposed to music, sport, and language, and having the confidence to network, as well as the promise of a new path beyond the *gaokao*—the future of the post-2010s generation is bright. Like the post-1995 teens, they will likely have more space and opportunity to experiment with different paths, use their own creativity, and leverage their networks. They will no doubt be criticized for having short attention spans and for being addicted to their digital devices, but they are also more likely to be the most articulate, open-minded and independent generation in the history of China.

KEY TAKEAWAYS
Parents of young kids today are on a journey of discovery with their children:
- They want to share fun and fresh experiences, but also have opportunities to learn with their kids
- They are looking for new experiential events, venues, and excursions that deliver entertainment for the whole family
- Travel and tourism is becoming a big part of this need to "discover together" as parents seek out new kid-friendly destinations that stimulate curiosity and exposure to different environments, cultures, and cuisines

Education is still king:
- Learning is a part of every activity, even in subtle ways
- Even in fun and play, parents want to "guide" their children toward tangible learning experiences
- Parents increasingly value "learning by doing"—both to make learning more engaging and to help kids acquire more useful daily life skills

- Structured and organized playtime is favored, and parents hope to see their children acquire new skills from play—including language and cognitive skills, but also "soft skills" like creativity and communication

Don't compete against others, compete against yourself:

- Parents don't see themselves as pushing or pressuring their kids, they see themselves as providing opportunities
- Even if parents feel social pressure for their children to keep up with other kids, they don't want their child to feel external pressure
- Parents want to guide their children towards activities that create internal pressure and drive—to help kids cultivate their own sense of ambition and achievement

Glossary

Post-80s/post-90s etc.

- These translated terms refer to successive generations of Chinese born in each decade, and can be somewhat confusing in English. In Chinese, the terms read "80后" "90后" and so on, meaning "born after 1980" or "born after 1990." The "post-80s" generation is therefore those born 1980-1989, the first decade for which this term scheme was used. "Post-80s" is roughly equivalent to "millennials" in the Western context, and older Chinese ascribe to them many of the same traits, such as supposed unreliability, a certain sense of entitlement, and so on. The popularity of the term "post-80s" led to similar terms being used to describe later generations.

One-child policy

- The widely-known "one-child policy" has had profound effects on Chinese demographics, which this book touches on numerous times. Basic details of the policy are useful to know. The policy was introduced in 1979, and restricted families from having more than one child. Enforcement was at times very strict, and included fines. Wealthier families wanting a second child sometimes simply opted to pay that fine. The policy also led to selective abortion, as many families, particularly in rural areas, preferred boys, leading a population imbalance with some 30 million extra males. For various reasons, authorities began to phase out the policy in 2015. Ethnic minorities were also historically subject to family planning policies, but often allowed more than one child.

Leftover women

- This term refers to women over 30 years of age that remain unmarried. Older women, and particularly those who are successful or highly educated, are considered undesirable for marriage. This is still a reality in China, but is changing very quickly, especially in major cities.

WeChat

- WeChat is the most popular messaging app in China, having recently surpassed one billion users. It is roughly similar to Whatsapp, but with much wider functionality. The app's mobile wallet in particular, which uses QR codes to facility payments, has helped fuel a revolution in mobile payments. Because of this payments service, and rival Alipay run by tech giant Alibaba, China may be on its way to becoming the first "cashless" society.

Weibo

- Weibo is a social media service similar to Twitter. Because of the popularity of WeChat, which has social media functionality, and increasing censorship of speech online, Weibo has declined in popularity.

Baidu

- Baidu is China's largest search engine.

Alibaba/Taobao

- Alibaba is an online retailer similar to Amazon that has arguably become China's best-known tech company. Taobao, Alibaba's consumer platform, has driven a massive shift to online shopping, and through promotions such as "Single's Day," held annually on November 11th, has become a cultural phenomenon. Alibaba subsidiary Ant Financial runs the company's mobile payments service Alipay.

JD.com

- JD.com is an online retailer and main competitor to Alibaba in online shopping.

Tencent

- Tencent is a technology giant and maker of many popular online services, including WeChat, and before that QQ, another messenger.

Guanxi

- This term refers to the network of relationships people have, especially in business and the government. If someone is said to "have a lot of *guanxi*," it means they have close relationships with powerful people.

Great Leap Forward

- The Great Leap Forward was a political campaign lasting from 1958-1962, meant to quickly modernize the economy. As a consequence of many factors, notably politically-driven policy mistakes, the campaign led to a famine estimated to have killed tens of million of people.

Cultural Revolution

- The Cultural Revolution was a political campaign that lasted from 1966-1976, primarily directed at combating perceived political enemies of the state. The campaign was extremely disruptive to society at all levels.

Reform and Opening Up

- Reform and Opening Up was begun by paramount leader Deng Xiaoping in 1978 and continues to this day. Reform and Opening Up is the key policy driving China's economic rise, and has been updated and adapted many times.

KOL

- KOLs are so-called "Key Opinion Leaders" on Chinese social media. They are popular figures that are coopted to promote products and serve as brand ambassadors.

Dai gou

- *Dai gou* is a shopping practice whereby customers place orders with people traveling abroad who purchase overseas goods. The practice is popular for many reasons, including taxes on some goods, and to ensure quality of certain products such as baby formula.

Bibliography

Anxious Wealth: Money and Morality Amongst China's New Rich
— John Osburg, 2013

The Giant Baby Nation (巨婴国)
— Wu Zhihong, 2016

China's Economy: What Everyone Needs to Know
— Arthur Kroeber, 2016

China's Crony Capitalism: the Dynamics of Regime Decay
— Minxin Pei, 2016

Fragile Elite, The Dilemmas of China's Top University Students
— Susanne Bregnbæk, 2016

Alibaba: The House that Jack Ma Built
— Duncan Clark

Red Obsession (film)
— Warrick Ross, David Roach, 2013

www.ingramcontent.com/pod-product-compliance
Lightning Source LLC
Chambersburg PA
CBHW011238120626
46549CB00009B/3319